Whole Person Librarianship

Whole Person Librarianship

A Social Work Approach to Patron Services

Sara K. Zettervall and Mary C. Nienow

LIBRARIES UNLIMITED®
An Imprint of ABC-CLIO, LLC
Santa Barbara, California • Denver, Colorado

Library of Congress Cataloging-in-Publication Data

Names: Zettervall, Sara K., author. | Nienow, Mary C., author.
Title: Whole person librarianship : a social work approach to patron services / Sara K. Zettervall and Mary C. Nienow.
Description: Santa Barbara, California : Libraries Unlimited, [2019] | Includes bibliographical references and index.
Identifiers: LCCN 2019020672 (print) | LCCN 2019980955 (ebook) | ISBN 9781440857768 (paperback) | ISBN 9781440857775 (ebook)
Subjects: LCSH: Libraries and community—United States. | Public services (Libraries)—United States. | Public services (Libraries)—United States—Case studies. | Librarians—Professional relationships—United States. | Library employees—Professional relationships—United States. | Social workers—Professional relationships—United States. | Social service—United States.
Classification: LCC Z716.4 .Z45 2019 (print) | LCC Z716.4 (ebook) | DDC 025.50973—dc23
LC record available at https://lccn.loc.gov/2019020672
LC ebook record available at https://lccn.loc.gov/2019980955

ISBN: 978-1-4408-5776-8 (paperback)
      978-1-4408-5777-5 (ebook)

23 22 21 20 19   1 2 3 4 5

This book is also available as an eBook.

Libraries Unlimited
An Imprint of ABC-CLIO, LLC

ABC-CLIO, LLC
147 Castilian Drive
Santa Barbara, California 93117
www.abc-clio.com

This book is printed on acid-free paper ∞

Manufactured in the United States of America

Contents

Preface

The collaboration that ultimately resulted in this book began in the summer of 2012. Sara was almost done with library school and was working on a practicum to lead a book club for a group of Somali girls. In planning for this work, the library system's community liaison outlined some challenging issues that could arise during book discussions. Would the girls talk about the lingering effects of civil war trauma in their families? Would they share frustrations they felt with older generations who pulled them toward more traditional ways? Sara's practicum supervisor kept reminding the liaison, "Sara's not a social worker." However, Sara thought, "I know some social workers who enjoy working with young people." So she invited Mary to co-lead the book club with her.

Although we, Mary and Sara, had been friends for years, our book club planning conversations were the first time we'd been prompted to talk seriously about our professions. As a student, Sara was steeped in the library school culture of learning to connect people with resources. She'd learned a lot about gathering and organizing electronic and physical materials, as well as how to make them appealing to different audiences, but was beginning to realize she lacked some skills for working with the people on the other side of those transactions. One of the first things Mary told her social workers do is "serve the whole person," paying attention to the multitude of factors impacting individuals in society, especially those who are vulnerable and often oppressed due to their race, religion, gender, or economic status. As Sara learned more, she realized this framework would be highly beneficial in librarianship as well. This is how the concept of Whole Person Librarianship (WPL) was born.

As we continued our conversations well beyond the book club, our curiosity was piqued: was anyone else in librarianship collaborating with social workers? Sara discovered a handful of urban libraries with social workers on staff, but there was very little written information available about these programs. In 2013, Sara's friend and library colleague Paul Lai helped her develop and run a blog exploring and explaining library-social work collaboration and its implications for our professions. The timing was right to be pioneers in bringing people from this nascent community together, and that blog eventually became Whole Person Librarianship (www.wholeperson librarianship.com), which is now the world's online hub for information, connection, and conversation around library-social work collaboration. Eventually, Paul retreated from regular participation, and we, Sara and Mary, were asked to present on and then write about the topic, leading to where we are today. Throughout, we continued to develop the concept of WPL to encompass both the practicalities of collaborating (who makes a good partner? how do we get started?) and the ways social work ideas can be applied to improve public service in libraries. Both parts of WPL, practice and concepts, are explored throughout this book.

The chapters in this book are arranged to guide readers from a basic understanding of the intersection of librarianship and social work through various stages of collaboration and into more complex social work concepts as they can apply to library service. Our primary audience is librarians and library staff, but we believe many social workers will also find this information interesting and useful. The book's content is structured around a nationwide survey, a series of focus groups, and one-on-one interviews we conducted in 2017 and 2018. This is all original research, supplemented by cited additional articles and news items (which have been the primary way of finding out about new collaborations). The quotes you will read are from practicing librarians, library staff members, social workers, and related professionals who are engaged in collaborative work. With a few exceptions, which are noted in the text, we have changed their names and the names of their libraries in order to give them the freedom to speak openly about their experiences. We're eternally grateful for the honesty and enthusiasm they brought to participating in this book, which wouldn't exist without their contributions.

Terminology

Every profession has its own jargon and ways of talking about its work that can be difficult for outsiders to understand. Librarianship and social work are no different, and we've tried throughout this book to define unfamiliar terms or concepts. In the case of acronyms, such as ALA for American Library Association, we introduce the full name once and then use the acronym for the rest of the book.

There are also familiar terms we've been thoughtful about using. We chose to use the common term "patrons" for people who come to the library for help; social workers would call those same individuals "clients." Because this book is written primarily for a library audience, we most often stick to using "patrons." The exceptions are times when we are writing about a distinctly social work situation or perspective, in which case we say "client." Similarly, we've taken care in how we refer to librarians and social workers. Not all library staff are librarians, so we try to avoid using "librarian" as a catch-all term. When the concepts and activities we discuss can apply to anyone working in a library, we say "library staff." When they are more specific to the type of work usually done by librarians, we say "librarian." We also try to distinguish other roles with terms like front-facing staff, public service staff, managers, and administrators.

On the social work side of things, there are actually some legal restrictions on who can be called a social worker, limited by licensure and academic degrees. We tried to be respectful of this, but we didn't check everyone's credentials and followed the lead of each participant who self-identified as a social worker. We do use the term "social worker" more loosely to refer to people in the community who are doing the kinds of work social workers do, whether or not the actual people involved are licensed. People doing work in the library are called "library social workers" regardless of credentials as well. However, in circumstances where we know libraries might be partnering with entities providing social services, but not necessarily social workers, we do say "social services" or "social service providers."

United States Perspective

Because the United States is the birthplace of library-social work collaboration in its current form, and because it's the territory most familiar to the authors, we speak primarily to and from an American perspective in this book. Canada was an early adopter as well, and Canadians continue to be important partners in this work. Where we feel confident to do so, we try to acknowledge this by speaking of North America more broadly. We avoid including examples from Canada and other nations not from a place of erasure but to ensure we don't make any false statements about regions outside our area of expertise. We also want to note Australian libraries have a great deal of interest in this work and seem poised to join us in it very soon. We were privileged to present about this topic at an international conference in Zagreb, Croatia, and met with interested librarians there as well. We look forward to sharing these connections around the world as knowledge of library-social work collaboration continues to grow.

Appendixes and Online Resources

To supplement each chapter, our website includes additional resources you can access to go deeper into the material presented (www.wholeperson librarianship.com/book/resources). We developed and tested many of these resources with audiences as a part of our conference sessions, keynotes, workshops, and technical assistance provided to librarians and systems across the United States over the past several years. Static items such as worksheets are typically included as appendixes and as printable versions online. Because we recognize even links to stable content can change quickly, electronic resources are typically listed only online. The website displays resources organized by chapter, which we will periodically review and update. In addition to our links, a comment section for each chapter allows you to add more links, book recommendations, and resources you think other readers may find helpful.

Introduction
Sister Professions

I wanted to be a librarian as my second career because I'm kind of drawn to that part of the service that libraries do. Not that I think librarians are social workers, but there is a similarity in how you can connect people with community services.

—Chue, public librarian

A Little Bit of History

Social work and libraries in the United States share a common historical origin. Both developed in the late 1800s as a response to the Progressive Era sentiment sweeping the country, as well as the increasing industrialization and immigration into the United States. Middle-class, European American women, educated but still confined to the roles of wife, mother, and homemaker, embraced an opportunity to participate and lead in civic, community, and occupational life. As they developed, librarianship and social work as professions were still dominated by men in leadership and administrative roles, but women comprised the rank-and-file workers. Women provided the vision, implementation, and sustainability of services to patrons, families, communities, and organizations.

In social work, the profession developed with a dual, often-competing focus. Charitable giving in the mid-19th century moved from being the responsibility of the family, small town, or church community to more formal regional and state organizations known as Charity Organization Societies (COS; Trattner 2007). The COS emerged in the middle of the 19th century as a response to the growing poverty, overcrowding, mental illness, alcoholism, and family dysfunction seen in growing urban areas. Members of the COS embraced the new trend of applying science to the human experience and sought to study and analyze the causes of poverty and other social problems. The COS was particularly focused on the individual or family and their inherent dysfunction. The solutions they designed, which came to be known as "interventions," were focused on helping the individual or family adapt to the environment and the prevailing norms and values of the dominant culture. This model—focusing on the individual or family and providing support in the form of case management, direct services, and therapy—remains the predominant model of social work today (Nienow 2017).

However, at the same time as the COS began providing social services, a contrasting model also developed. The Settlement House movement represented a community-based approach to prevalent social problems of the day. Settlement houses were often large homes purchased by middle-class individuals, located within impoverished, immigrant neighborhoods. The most famous and well-known was Hull House, owned and operated by Jane Addams, who is considered one of the founders of the profession of social work. Individuals who were interested in working with the community on pressing social issues lived in the settlement house, which served as both their place of residence and work. Settlement houses offered a variety of services to the community, such as English language learning; kindergartens; classes on art, literature, or other instructional seminars; and workshops focused on development of specific skills such as sewing, cooking, or bookbinding (Tung 2014). Residents at the settlement houses also helped to organize their neighbors for important political reforms to laws and policies. Some examples include labor regulations, sanitation, housing codes, and resistance to the corruption of law enforcement and governmental officials. The settlement house model of social service provision focused on adapting and changing the environment to help meet the needs of the individual, family, or community. This model of social service work is not as dominant as the one developed by the COS but is still an integral part of all social work education and contributes to the social work practice of seeing and understanding the person-in-environment (PIE), a concept we explore in chapter 1. A small number of social workers still engage in this kind of practice and can be found in positions of community organization, government, and administration.

In the late 19th century, around the same time as the COS and settlement houses began shaping what would become social work, Andrew Carnegie began funding library buildings throughout the United States and across the world. This formed the foundation of our current expectation of a public library in every community and an open research library in every university. Melvil Dewey also founded the American Library Association (ALA), *Library Journal*, and the first library school at Columbia College in the same decade Jane Addams founded Hull House. Like social workers, many early librarians, especially in community-embedded public libraries, welcomed immigrants and the poor into their spaces and offered services to help acclimate them to the dominant culture. Just one example was Edith Guerrier, an early-20th century librarian in Boston, who created "Saturday Evening Girls" clubs: "Observing that the intellectual capacities and development of young immigrant women were essentially overlooked, Guerrier shaped these groups so as to provide this disenfranchised cohort with exposure to the core elements one would have encountered in a progressive liberal arts education" (Bausman 2016). Today's librarians who are invested in community outreach and engagement can easily recognize themselves in this work and may find it heartening to be reminded this has been a strand of librarianship from its inception. At the same time, it serves as a caution that support services can easily cross the line from education to assimilation.

As significant as progressive movements were to both professions, and as much as they present models for a continuation of the sisterhood of social work and librarianship in contemporary settings, they also share significant disparities typical of that time period. Like social work, librarianship at the time was staffed—and in many ways shaped—by women, but at its highest levels it was dominated by men. Dewey, whose name is still taught to most schoolchildren as part of learning to use a library, was a notorious misogynist and racist (Ford 2018a). For many decades, the Library of Congress was the bulwark around a white, male, classist, heterocentric perspective in cataloging, though it was eventually besieged by Sanford Berman's insistence on equitable revision of subject headings. Those same Carnegie libraries standing in many communities to this day often refused admission to African American patrons. We intentionally call out "dominant culture" in this historical summary because both social work and librarianship upheld the values of the dominant culture, prioritizing them over the values, people, and ideas of other cultures also present during these times. Early efforts in both professions improved countless lives but did so from a moralistic and narrow belief about the "best way" to live. Both social work and librarianship currently engage in significant discussion on how to overcome these legacies but have yet to find effective solutions that permanently shift our deeply ingrained professional cultures.

Current Statistics

Public librarians are fond of pointing out there are more libraries than McDonald's in the United States (and it's true [Back 2018]), but there are nearly five times as many professional social workers as there are librarians in the United States. Social workers numbered 682,100 in 2016, while librarians totaled 138,200 (US Bureau of Labor Statistics 2018a, 2018b). And yet, with the exception of the occasional appearance by child protection in a police procedural TV show, social workers are rarely visible in the public sphere. Because librarians are still very much associated with the physical edifice of the library and the materials contained within, and because so much library work happens in view of the community, they can seem much more present than social workers. However, social work is entwined with nearly every support system in society, a fact we will explore more in chapter 1.

Contemporary librarianship and social work carry forward the effects of their history as "women's work" with significant female majorities: 82.5% of social workers are women, while 79.5% of librarians are women (US Bureau of Labor Statistics 2018a, 2018b). A recent study of academic libraries shows women continue to lag behind men in pay and are less likely to negotiate higher salaries until they reach positions of power (Silva and Galbraith 2018), while library administrative and management positions continue to skew male in extreme disproportion to the population's overall gender makeup. Concerning racial identity, social workers do somewhat better: 70% of them are white, versus 86% of librarians. The remaining social workers are 24% black, 4% Asian, and 14% Hispanic, as compared to librarians, who are 5% Asian and 10% Hispanic but only 6% black. We are curious, given how similar the rest of our histories and current statistics are, why black social workers are noticeably more numerous than black librarians. It may be the result of social work's persistent adherence to social justice ideals, but we can't know for sure based on surface data and would be interested in follow-up, comparative studies.

Regardless of their differences, though, these statistics reveal discrepancies between both professions and the populations they serve. This provides context for understanding the importance of institutional accountability (explored more fully in chapter 6), which is critical when working with vulnerable populations. Differences can get in the way of service and need to be revealed and examined, repeatedly and with humility, by those of us holding positional power. This is something we stress throughout the book, and we encourage readers to delve into the many complementary publications and learning opportunities available regarding social justice and equity work in libraries. We provide some recommended starting points in this chapter's online resources.

Shared Ethics

Reflecting our common heritage, librarianship and social work share significant overlap in our professional ethics. These ethics guide and influence the way we behave in the field, prioritize and structure tasks, and make decisions. Sometimes, where these ethics lead to different choices, they can prompt misunderstandings. However, we encourage readers to consider these as opportunities to learn more about each other. Because of the influence our ethics have in every part of our working lives, we'll be referencing them throughout the book. Links to national and international library and social work codes of ethics are provided in this chapter's online resources.

Service

In the United States, both librarianship and social work list service as their number-one priority. The shared motivation to provide excellent service to patrons and clients is a key reason these two professions work so well together. The primary difference worth noting in a library-social work context is that the National Association of Social Workers' (NASW) Code of Ethics focuses on the most vulnerable members of society: "Social Workers' primary goal is to help people in need" (NASW 2018). Librarianship grapples with the challenges of providing service to "all library users" by defining service in terms of "equitable access" and "accurate, unbiased, and courteous responses to all requests" (ALA 2017). Librarians are constantly assessing who is and is not using the library and how to shape current collections and programs to meet those needs. Social workers look at the same set of people and ask, instead: Who in our population would benefit from extra effort to set them on equal ground with everyone else? The answer to this question focuses their efforts on those individuals, communities, or populations. This makes social workers great partners to librarians who want to provide more equitable policies and services, but library staff members may need to remind themselves from time to time that social workers purposely focus on particular patrons and don't think of serving everyone in the same way as librarians. Similarly, social workers may need to keep in mind librarians need to work with a wide range of people, not just the ones who need the most help.

Privacy and Confidentiality

Social workers and librarians both prioritize patron/client privacy as a core ethic, but they diverge in the different types of information they collect and store. Librarians "protect each user's right to privacy and confidentiality" (ALA 2017), such that many libraries refuse to collect and save more information than what is minimally required to set up a user account. In contrast, social workers collect a great deal of sensitive information as a necessary step to form a detailed understanding of their clients and develop an intervention. Social workers also need to be mindful of how that information informs their view of clients, so their professional ethics remind them to "respect the inherent dignity and worth of [every] person" (NASW 2018). While protective of client privacy, social workers are mandated by the NASW Code of Ethics (and often state law) to break confidentiality if they believe clients will harm themselves or others. Social workers are also considered "mandated reporters," which means if they suspect anyone of harming a vulnerable adult, or a child under 18, they must report this information to the appropriate authority. Mandated reporting is so embedded in social work that it can be confusing for social workers to learn librarians often aren't mandated reporters (and may not even be familiar with the term). Librarians have even been known to go to court to avoid sharing patron records. These differences in professional ideals create some need for negotiation between librarians and social workers, which we explore in greater depth in the section on data collection in chapter 4.

Access to Information

For librarians, providing access to information is a key priority, and the process of discovering accurate and complete information forms the basis of the library–patron relationship. However, the mandate to "resist all efforts to censor library resources" (ALA 2017) means librarians won't always agree with the content of their collections, and they remain mindful at all times that their role is provision of information rather than interpretation of content. For social workers, providing access to information is more about navigating a confusing system of services, so they "recognize the central importance of human relationships" (NASW 2018). As part of this process, social workers often have to translate information for clients and help them make sense of the information they procure on a variety of topics from parenting to dementia—a type of expertise that stands in contrast to the way librarians intentionally place responsibility for interpretation on the patron. Both librarians and social workers should be aware of these different boundaries in order to support each other's professional integrity. In fact, as we explore throughout the book, the organizational skills librarians develop around access to information can be a tremendous help and complementary service to the complex relationship networks formed by social workers.

Respect for Rights

Librarianship and social work are both invested in supporting the rights of the populations they serve. We already visited the social work ethic of "dignity and worth of the person," and the International Federation of Social Workers (IFSW) also prioritizes "promoting the right to self-determination" (IFSW 2018). Clients have the right to define their own goals; to accept or decline services; and to give voice to their needs, wants, and desires. Librarians also value self-determination, though they do so by providing thoughtful collections that enable each patron to steer their own course of discovery. Social workers are fierce advocates for basic human rights and strive to ensure everyone has access to these rights, no matter their race, gender identification, physical or intellectual ability, religious belief, nationality, or economic status. Librarians are also dogged in defense of patron rights, but as in other areas, this is done with careful attention to everyone involved, as in advocating "balance between the interests of information users and rights holders" (ALA 2017). Social workers face a gray area when their client is a vulnerable adult, child, or someone whose rights have been legally revoked (e.g., prisoners). In these situations, they may find themselves acting in a role of enforcing laws and judicial decisions that impose upon the rights of the client but support ethical responsibility to the broader society. Social workers have given a great deal of thought and attention to human rights, and we devote chapter 5 to exploring what librarians can learn from social workers about defending the rights of patrons.

Professional Skills and Integrity

The NASW Code of Ethics states "social workers act honorably and responsibly" (NASW 2018), which means social workers must be as transparent as possible with all aspects of their work. Social workers continuously seek out accurate, evidence-based information, and they practice only within their area of training and expertise. When they discover their clients need assistance outside their particular area of expertise, they're required to seek out help from others. One of social work's six core values includes competence, so operating within the scope of their practice expertise is critical. Librarians may recognize that this is similar to their call to "distinguish between our personal convictions and professional duties and not allow our personal beliefs to interfere with fair representation of the aims of our institutions or the provision of access to their information resources" (ALA 2017). Librarians also learn to take care not to offer advice in areas where they don't have expertise, the classic example being the patron seeking medical guidance, whom the librarian instructs on resources to navigate to their own answers. In this respect, both professions require a high level of self-awareness and humility, asking practitioners to recognize the extent of their abilities and be willing to make their limitations known to their patrons or clients, supervisors, and colleagues. In chapter 6, we explore how social workers cultivate self-awareness and humility and how librarians can apply these concepts to their work.

Social Justice

We conclude this section by highlighting social justice because it's the heart of social work—"social workers challenge social injustice" (NASW 2018)—and it's the motivation behind many librarians' commitment to their work, even as it can sometimes be controversial within the profession as a whole. Regardless of how or where they're employed, social workers strive to eliminate oppression and discrimination, and to make society's distribution of resources like housing and education as equitable as possible. Social workers recognize many of the problems facing society today come from institutions and policies grounded in power differentials, which prioritize those with money, status, ability, or physical strength. Social workers aim to ensure all people can live where their basic needs are met, their capacities are recognized, and their voices and perspectives are part of every decision impacting upon them. Regardless of the controversy some see in library activism—a topic we touch on in chapter 5—librarians do amazing work in service of social justice every day. The "textbook" example we've been using in workshops of a social justice effort is the Ferguson (Missouri) Municipal Public Library's response to racial unrest after the police shooting of Michael Brown in 2014. The director of the library received a number of national awards for the extraordinary community engagement efforts he coordinated at his library (ALA 2015). We believe the collaborations explored in this book support the central place of social justice in librarianship as well as social work.

Growth of Library-Social Work Collaboration

In 2009, San Francisco Public Library (SFPL) took action in response to patron needs in a way no library had done before: they hired a full-time social worker to their library staff. Leah Esguerra[1] became the first library social worker and began groundbreaking work that would be emulated in dozens of libraries over the following decade (we explore this model in chapter 4). Leah's position was established to address the significant, visible population of patrons experiencing homelessness using SFPL's downtown library as a day shelter. The challenge presented by patrons sleeping, bathing, making phone calls, eating, and even having sex in the library isn't new, but the scope of the situation in San Francisco, which has one of the highest per capita rates of people experiencing homelessness in the United States, felt especially pressing to library staff. SFPL wasn't alone in its need to serve these patrons. Of the 38 news items we reviewed about libraries hiring social workers, published between 2014 and 2018, over 75% indicated a primary reason for those hires was the presence of a visible population of people experiencing homelessness in the library.[2]

Since 2009, the number of libraries participating in social work collaborations has grown dramatically. When we started the WPL blog in 2013, there were a handful of programs in place. San José Public Library pioneered the placement of social work students in libraries (Estreicher 2013), while Winnipeg, Canada, was an early adopter of the SFPL model (CBC News 2013).

---

1. Real name.
2. We performed this environmental scan in September 2018. Articles used for the scan can be found in the interactive map at www.wholepersonlibrarianship.com.

Public libraries in Washington, D.C., Edmonton, Philadelphia, and Denver followed with their own hires in 2014 and 2015. In 2016, we created an interactive map on the WPL website to start tracking program locations and types, at which point the number had inched closer to 20, including social work students and social service "office hours" in libraries, as well as social workers who were hired to work in libraries. In 2018, the total number of all of these types of collaborations rose from around 50 at the start of the year to over 100 by the end. Most of that total is made up of full-time hires and social work student placements, but there are likely many collaborative programs to place social services in libraries for "office hours" or other arrangements we haven't tracked because they don't make news items or appear in research in the same ways. In this book's conclusion, we'll explore some emerging trends and developments we expect to see in the near future as a result of this rapid expansion.

In addition to the primary placement of library social workers in urban settings, many library-social work collaborations flourish in suburbs. Suburban areas have witnessed a growth of homelessness in the past 10 years. Alecia, who completed her MSW practicum in a suburban library, witnessed this firsthand: "People who are experiencing homelessness might not be as visible in the ways that some people expect a homeless person to present themselves. . . . I would hear people who worked at the library say they had no idea that person was in crisis or was living out of [a car], so they just assumed that they were a retired person who just had a lot of time to spend at the library, . . . and I think it was kind of two-fold, that patrons don't always recognize that librarians can help direct them to services that just aren't literature-based." This revelation of invisible community needs is a common "side effect" of placing social workers in libraries of all types and is something we'll touch on throughout the book, particularly when we discuss cultural humility in chapter 6. Because people experiencing homelessness in the suburbs and in exurban and rural areas tend to be less immediately visible, the library-as-sanctuary can play an especially significant role in helping people connect to services.

Libraries' mobilization to serve patrons experiencing homelessness can feel like a contemporary issue because much of it was prompted by the rise of internet access in libraries. The "traditional" library patron turned to the web instead of the reference desk for their research needs, while at the same time, internet terminals in libraries attracted patrons who couldn't afford the technology at home. For those experiencing homelessness or high mobility, the free internet access in libraries can be their only way to stay connected through social media to distant family members and friends. However, public libraries have long been the only safe, indoor space many people experiencing homelessness can find during the day. To give just one example, we came across an article from over 40 years ago on "the emerging environment of the urban main library," lamenting the influx of patrons experiencing poverty (Shaughnessy 1972). The ALA adopted Policy 61 on "Library Services to the Poor" in 1990 (Krier 2012). So, social workers in the library form a modern response to contemporary developments, but there's a history of responsive service in libraries and a wealth of information and training modules already available for staff to learn more about those who experience poverty and homelessness. We include some starting points in the online resources for this chapter.

Finally, while large urban libraries spearheaded the hire of library social workers and continue to serve as examples and guides for new collaborations, they're far from the only model in this expanding professional realm. This book not only details those major, transformative library-social work hires but also the many smaller and scalable ways collaborations can and do happen.

Online Resources

www.wholepersonlibrarianship.com/book/resources/intro

- Links to:
    - ALA, NASW, IFLA, and IFSW codes of ethics
    - ALA policy statement on "Library Services to the Poor"
    - Webinars about serving patrons experiencing homelessness in public libraries
- Interactive map of library-social work collaborations across the world
- Recommended books and articles to provide context on poverty, class, and race in the library profession
- Additional resources provided by you and your colleagues

CHAPTER ONE

Relationships Are the New Reference Collection

Public libraries are connectors in the community. What if what a patron needs is a connection to the community organization or anything else the community has to provide? We can be the expert in that too. And that's a hundred percent our role just as much as finding physical or digital materials for someone.

—Bella, homelessness and poverty librarian

Overview

One of the first questions we hear from both librarians and social workers when we introduce them to the concept of WPL is: Are you trying to turn librarians into social workers? The answer is an emphatic no! As we established in the introduction, librarians and social workers have highly complementary, but distinct, approaches to patron/client services. Librarians call on social workers to fill a gap they feel acutely in the needs of patrons, but the role of librarians in meeting those needs remains information-based.

In the introduction, we covered the shared foundations of librarianship and social work. In this chapter, we shift into a contemporary, practical perspective to ask: What role do social workers and social service agencies play in communities? Where does the library fit into those roles? How can library staff turn understanding into connections with community partners?

This chapter has two goals: first, to inform library staff who aren't familiar with social work about the basics of what social workers do; and second, to provide context and confidence for library staff to create their own "relationship-based reference collection" of social services in their community.

To that end, we begin with Sara's story of using relationships to support community-embedded library work. We then offer practical descriptions of types of social work, along with a worksheet to begin identifying community social services. We conclude by explaining some basic social work concepts that are useful for understanding a social work approach and applying it to library services. The approaches we describe in this chapter form a foundation for libraries to prepare for the opportunities presented throughout the book.

Sara's Story

Sara Zettervall,[1] coauthor of this book, works as a community embedded librarian at the Cedar Riverside Opportunity Center (CROC). The neighborhood of Cedar Riverside packs nearly 8,000 people into a few blocks near downtown Minneapolis, and most of those residents are East African immigrants and refugees. Many are Somali, but a significant number are Oromo, an ethnic group from Ethiopia who have their own separate culture and language. Sara serves these immigrants as a public librarian through Hennepin County Library, but she doesn't work in a traditional library space. Instead, the library is one partner in a collaborative office focused on education and job readiness for residents of the Cedar Riverside neighborhood. At CROC, the primary tenant is an employment services nonprofit, EMERGE. The library provides two full-time staff to deliver educational programs and services. Other partners in the space include Hennepin County more broadly; the City of Minneapolis, which funds a full-time Somali community coordinator; and Minneapolis College, which supports recruitment, enrollment, and funding leading to career-specific credentials.

One of the main priorities for CROC from its opening in early 2017 has been to increase employment among young people from the community. With high unemployment among young men in particular, CROC's partnering organizations were eager to find a way to connect them to opportunities. Sara explained, "EMERGE provides career prep things like resume help, GED classes, job readiness for immigrants, and Minnesota Family Investment Program (MFIP) coordinators . . . providing welfare-to-work service for families." These services, along with those provided by the City of Minneapolis and Minneapolis College, primarily reach adults. All of the partners support and help to promote each other's programs. They also share connections with various other groups and individuals in the community, including mosques, Somali TV, and youth sports programs. Sara's first priority as a librarian shaping her new role was to build those relationships. She

---

1. Sara's story uses real names.

explained, "At first, I just tried to be present as much as possible. This is a very word-of-mouth community, and a lot of the most important connections I made at first happened just by being around when people stopped by [the offices]."

Within the CROC framework, the library has a special role to play in connecting with teenagers and younger youth. It entered the collaboration at CROC with a promise to support youth employment through a Teen Tech Squad, mentored by Sara. Teen Tech Squads exist at several libraries throughout the Hennepin County Library system, but the CROC squad was the first to be placed in a shared space outside a library building. Squad members are paid a living wage, and each team employs four high schoolers. They design their own workshops on STEAM (science, technology, engineering, arts, and math) topics, then offer them to younger youth in the community. They also benefit from special career and personal development opportunities. Not only does this mean fair pay and life skills preparation for neighborhood youth, but it also benefits the library system by bringing more diverse and community-reflecting voices into staff. For Sara, it has also been an opportunity to engage in WPL: "We're really encouraged to think about every aspect of [the teens'] success, so it's not just about technology skills but supporting their confidence and place in the world."

The other anchor program for the library has been HCL's Homework Help, which also follows a format and structure developed for use in libraries across the system. Sara said, "We didn't know right away that we were going to do Homework Help. We went in saying, we have some good things planned, but we also want to hear what community members have to say about what they need from us. We heard over and over: homework assistance." A community organization across the street had been providing after-school tutoring for K–12 students but lost its funding shortly after CROC opened. The timing was right for the library, which was already planning to expand Homework Help, to step in and fill the gap. Sara said that development was beneficial not just as a response to community requests but also a way to build relationships and a sense of belonging: "It has brought people from the community into that space in a way that makes them feel really comfortable there. It's been a really good way to connect with adults as well because a lot of the time, the moms in particular will bring their kids to Homework Help and to do after-school activities, and then the adults will hang around with us." The kids who come for Homework Help also make a built-in audience for Teen Tech Squad programs.

The library's initial focus was to work with older teens, but Sara said this is an audience that takes more time to grow. Young men in the community in particular are underemployed, she explained, "so there was a lot of interest coming into the space in working with young men. That's the part that's really challenging. I mean, it's a lot easier to be like, 'Hey kids, come in here and do your homework.' The moms are like, 'Hurray, kids! Go in there and do your homework, and they'll have some enrichment activities for you!' It's a lot harder to figure out how to connect with 17, 18, and 19-year-old guys." Sara said they are hopeful the programs will eventually help support and connect with some of those harder-to-reach teens. She explained, "It's just a lesson in patience and timing and, of course, going back to being present and just being available so that you're there, and you have those relationships in place when the right moment comes."

One of the ways the library has addressed this challenge is by hiring Abshir Omar to be its Somali community liaison, working in tandem with Sara on all programming. Abshir's history in and strong ties to Cedar River-side allowed him to quickly establish rapport with the residents, both young and old. Abshir's role is crucial to the library's relationship-based approach. Sara explained,

> [The library system] was really intentional about creating a position in the community liaison that would be a peer employee for the librarian. It's different than what we're used to because, in branch libraries, the librarian doesn't really have this type of peer. There are people that are doing work that's more support work, and there are supervisors, but there aren't non-librarians that are at the same level. So it's a really different situation to be working in, and we had to do some work together to figure out, okay, what's different about what each of us does? What knowledge set do I bring versus what Abshir brings? Then also working closely with these community service providers and figuring out what the library can provide that will be helpful to them. It's always a work in progress.

Another unique facet of CROC is the lack of a physical collection. Without many books or other materials on hand, Sara finds there's still much to share. "The library offers so much, and a lot of it is stuff that people don't know about. There's so much online these days, and that's where I've been trying to work really hard to think about: how can we help people in the space understand what the library has to provide in that respect?" An example Sara gave was working with Minneapolis College so prospective students know they can take free practice college placement exams online through the library. Similarly, Sara said she is working with EMERGE to help its GED students access practice tests and tutoring online. Homework Help also has an online component with a live connection to tutors. Sara summarized her expertise in implementing this model: "There are a lot of ways the library is prepared to support the community, and then it's really up to me to figure out how to make those connections. That's definitely something that as a librarian I can bring to the table right away."

Sara also attributes much of the success of library programming to the partners with whom they collaborate. She said the partners in the space have been "so useful in promoting our events, especially when we were getting started up, because they were the ones who had people of necessity coming in from the community to talk to them, and families especially with the MFIP coordinators. So for us to then say, can you share with your families that we're going to start having this after-school activity, that was something they were really happy to share because they knew people wanted it. It was also very beneficial to us to be able to get people coming in."

The library's successes at CROC have been accompanied by efforts that didn't last but provided good learning opportunities. Sara shared the example of Conversation Circles, which were intended to support English language learning for adults. Sara explained, "Typically, in our library system, those are led by volunteers. But we decided in this case I would lead it as a staff member because it was a good way for me to meet people from the community and have a chance to talk to them. Ultimately, that was not a sustainable project for us, but it did end up being a really good way for me to have some more in-depth conversations with community members about what was going on and start to do some of that relationship-building, too."

The library wants its programming to be responsive to the community needs, but it has to balance that desire with specific goals it shares with partners in the space. Also, two library staff have to be more careful than a building full of staff about how they commit their time. As Sara said, "You have to be a little bit creative sometimes if you think about how you want to respond to people asking about things." For example, parents in the community would often want to know if the library was going to offer storytime or other early childhood programming. This wasn't within the library's immediate scope of work, but one way it was able to provide some resources was by turning the CROC reception area into an early literacy space. Sara explained,

> We noticed a lot of families were coming in to meet with folks in EMERGE, and they would bring their little kids with them because the preschool-aged kids would be with mom all day. They'd be in our waiting area with nothing for the kids to do. So now there are some picture books there. There are some games to play with [to make] words and different learning experiences. A lot of [how we respond] is thinking strategically about what is it we need to do within this space in relation to what is it that people are asking for.

One of the recent developments Sara shared is how engaged the youth in the community have been in advocating for their needs. A group of young men have come together and have been proactive in sharing, "There's not enough here for us. We need more." Not only are they expressing these needs to the library, but also to other community leaders. Sara said, "Abshir has been going to these meetings they've been having with people from the city, and they've had the mayor come to one of them, people from the police department coming to listen to what the young folks are saying they need for support. That's where I think we're hoping we'll be able to follow their lead and be at least part of a response to what they're asking."

When asked what kind of successes the program was able to demonstrate, Sara said:

> We named before any of this began that our goals were these very relationship-based things. So it was about community members feeling welcome in the space. It was about creating more of a sense of community. It was about providing support for some cultural programs, which we did and still do as well. We have numbers. We keep track of that stuff too. But I think it's been a lot of those personal stories that have been able to show the success of the library. Especially at first, that was super important. I mean, now we're getting more numbers. Now we're actually getting to the point where we have enough youth coming to Homework Help that it's becoming a little challenging to have our Teen Tech Squad programs and Homework Help in the same space. So that's a good challenge to have. But at first, when you have that patience and you have to really wait to get started up, the stories of those initial relationships and contacts you're building are super important.

What started out as an 18-month pilot program for a specific community in Minneapolis has become a permanent and thriving part of the county library system. The success of the programming has led the library not only to continue to fund both Sara and Abshir's positions but also to test out additional community-embedded positions that focus on other communities within the county. Sara said all their programming at CROC is part of an ongoing process of balancing "what the library is going to really, not just be able to provide, but also be able to provide in a sustainable way that's going to actually make an impact and a difference," along with being in touch with truly meeting the needs of patrons. Sara stated, "It's not just like we heard from people at the start this is what we want, and then we added some stuff, and then we're just sitting with it; it's constantly talking to people, constantly hearing what's going on. We continue to evolve over time based on what's there."

Building the Relationship-Based Reference Collection

In the title and opening quote of this chapter, we introduced the idea relationships are the new reference collection. Across our work with libraries interested in connecting with social services, we see library staff collecting, cultivating, and curating community relationships in much the same way librarians used to create ready reference collections. This model of relationship-building can be done by any library, regardless of whether they bring a social worker on site, and it's a natural extension of long-standing library traditions. As Chue, a librarian in a small urban system, noted,

> [One] way of looking at it is if you define information more flexibly, our library actually historically has done a really good job of things like lists of places where you can get free meals and lists of places where you can get housing information for people who have [been] experiencing homelessness in the local area. And that's information. It needs sometimes to be done less passively, where you actually do outreach and connection to get that information to people, but we've been doing that for years, so the staff is pretty advanced in some ways of doing these projects.

The significant difference between what libraries have already been doing and creating a true collection of relationships is the extra step of outreach and connection to community partners. In much the same way understanding how to use the index of a book grants access to the information inside, relationships with social service partners provide a key to the specific services patrons need, as well as a low-barrier point of entry for referrals.

The first step for library staff to build a relationship-based reference collection is understanding the basics of what social workers do. Staff will start at different levels—many folks will already know several social workers and have a solid understanding of what they provide, while others will only have a general sense of some of the kinds of social service agencies out there. That's just fine! When we started collaborating, we'd been friends for years, but Sara had very little idea of what social workers actually do (and Mary probably thought librarians read books all day). The point for libraries entering this work is that it's important to be nonjudgmental about what staff may or may not know, and bring everyone to at least a baseline knowledge of what social work is and what resources are part of the collection. In a traditional reference model, paraprofessional staff may or may not have known how to use complicated reference books, but they knew what kind of content was available in them in order to be effective in handing patrons over to librarians. Similarly, the relationship piece of the relationship-based reference collection may be assigned to librarians who are engaged in community outreach, but other staff should have a general knowledge of the partnering organizations involved in those relationships.

What Do Social Workers Do?

Social work is a broad profession dedicated to solving social and individual problems. Social workers can be found almost anywhere: hospitals, nursing homes, prisons, schools—and now libraries. At an individual level, the social worker's role is to work alongside the client to facilitate whatever change needs to happen in the client's life. Sometimes, that change happens by choice, like when a couple seeks to adopt a child. Other times, change is forced by a health crisis, like when a veteran with brain damage has a social worker case manager who coordinates the many health professionals involved in treatment; or by a legal mandate, like when a parent whose children have been placed in foster care has supervised visits with a social worker from child protective services. Regardless of the setting, social workers incorporate a strengths-based perspective in their work, treating the client as the expert who best understands their own needs. Social workers and clients work in partnership to identify the client's strengths and develop a plan together to address the client's goals.

While they're best known for their work with individuals and families, social workers also focus on social change to improve the lives of the people who are most vulnerable in our society. As we touched on in the introduction, social work is a values-based profession, guided by social justice to promote equity across all parts of society. Social workers are trained to engage in the political process, learning how to develop public policies and advocate for the well-being of the populations they serve. For example, Mary worked for several years in the Minnesota State Legislature, helping elected officials understand policy and budget items related to health and human services. After that, she ran an organization advocating for early care and education policies that supported children, families, and the childcare workforce. She shares more about those experiences in chapter 5 of this book, which delves into what library staff can learn from the ways social workers do advocacy.

Social workers like Mary who focus primarily on social change, work with communities, or help run organizations identify their work as "macro practice." On the other hand, social workers who work with individuals identify their work as "micro practice." In between those levels is work with families and groups, called "mezzo practice." Danelle, an urban librarian who is officially assigned to coordinate social service contacts, does a great job of describing what mezzo practice looks like: "I always say it's a good thing to know our neighbors. On one side we have Brooks Brothers, and on the other we have a church that has a shelter. So, we get lots of different types of people in our library, and we set up to try and connect them the best we can with information on social services." We'll explore micro-, mezzo-, and macro-level work in greater detail later in this chapter and repeatedly throughout the rest of the book. But for now, knowing the basics of how social workers conceptualize their work can help library staff identify the many types of services in their communities and classify them as resources.

Finally, it's important to remember social workers aren't miracle workers. While they have a broad range of skills, not all issues can be quickly resolved.

One of the core values of social work, the importance of human relationships, means social workers are focused on developing relationships that will help them work with clients in a meaningful way. However, not only does relationship-building take time, but it also depends on commitment from everyone involved. Librarians working with social workers should not expect them to come in and "solve" all the different concerns facing librarians' patrons. Beyond working with patrons, social workers can also offer training, consultation, and support to library staff who may encounter difficult situations their own training didn't prepare them to handle. We'll cover more information about that kind of support in chapter 4.

"I'm Not a Social Worker, but I Know Where to Find One"

The next step in creating a relationship-based reference collection is determining which social services are available in your community. As Elana, an urban public library director, noted, "A lot of [connecting with services] is about understanding what the resources are and where to find them and having somebody who is willing to help you navigate." Although these services are shaped by policymaking at the national and state levels, funding flows through multiple sources with varying purposes and foci. As a result, patrons who need access to these services face a complex matrix of support that crosses back and forth between government agencies, nonprofit organizations, and religion-based services. Even the social workers who, as case managers, are tasked with understanding and navigating those services, may have a hard time keeping track of them all.

Some examples of places to find social work partners include:

- **Government Agencies:** The many administrative divisions within government employ social workers at local, county, state, and national levels. One of the tricky things about finding the most appropriate agency for connection is that names can vary, even between city and county equivalents serving the same community. It's also the case that some localities place health services in the same division as social services, whereas others decide to separate them out. So you might have one Department of Health and Human Services, or one Department of Health and one Department of Human Services. Other names can include County Social Services, Public Health Department, Welfare Office, Social Services, or related terms. It's worth taking time to learn the structure of government agencies in your library's community and where they're the same and different across levels, as well as which offices handle different needs, such as mental health, physical health, child welfare, supportive housing, and unemployment benefits. Meet and talk to the people who work in these different agencies. The relationship-based collection librarian does not, and in fact should not, know the labyrinth of forms and procedures within each agency: that's what the social service provider helps the patron navigate after the handoff. The goal is a general understanding of the content of each resource.

- **Veterans Affairs (VA):** The VA is another government agency but is worth mentioning as a separate resource because it operates relatively independently. It employs a lot of social workers as case managers for veterans, who work closely with them to navigate their special benefits and supports. Because of these close relationships between case managers and veterans, there's less need for relationship-based collection librarians to know the divisions within the VA than within government agencies in general. VA staff often make great library partners, with an interest in both active outreach to veterans in the community and connecting veterans to library resources in innovative ways. In one example, Sara partnered with housing for formerly homeless veterans to embed library materials and programs on site, which has continued through the work of other librarians across time, in large part due to the commitment shown by service providers ("Home Is Where the Books Are" 2018). A larger-scale, very successful project we list as an online resource for this chapter is Veterans Connect @ the Library in California.

- **Hospital Libraries and Social Services:** Libraries located near hospitals may want to find out whether that hospital has a library with librarians on staff. Such medical libraries, which support providers' research and help patients find information on diagnoses, used to be much more common; in a post-internet world, even the ones remaining are often lightly staffed. Medical librarians may appreciate a connection to the local library. Similarly, hospital case workers who don't have the support of an in-house library may appreciate a reciprocal relationship. In addition to getting to know hospital social service coordinators, libraries can tap the National Network of Libraries of Medicine (NNLM), which offers robust outreach programs to educate public and academic librarians on medical resources.

- **College or University Social Work Department:** We'll discuss connecting to a local school of social work more extensively in chapter 3. But even if the library doesn't intend to host a social work intern anytime soon, it can be useful to know which degrees are offered and where, and to make a connection to the department chair or field coordinator. Connections at the school can help raise awareness among social workers of the library as a place to connect to resources, and librarians and social workers can also share a high-level view of needs and concerns in the community.

- **National Association for Mental Illness (NAMI) State Chapter:** NAMI is a great source for basic staff training on mental health issues, and its site is a good starting point for identifying and cataloging local mental health agencies and providers.

- **National Association of Social Workers (NASW) State Chapter:** Although NASW services exist primarily to support social workers as professionals in the field, some are beginning to form interest groups around library-social work collaboration. It may be worth reaching out to your state's NASW chapter to see whether it's active in the community and find out whether there's existing interest in building connections. We also discuss possible growth within professional organizations in the conclusion chapter.

- **Faith-Based Organizations:** In many locations, social services have evolved over time such that government, nonprofit, and faith-based offerings are inextricably intertwined. For example, where we live in Minneapolis and St. Paul, services to people experiencing homelessness are provided in large part by Catholic Charities and Lutheran Social Services. This dates back to before the New Deal, when virtually all services were provided by nongovernment entities. The involvement of religious organizations can be a challenge for libraries, which are right to be concerned about aligning or even appearing to align with any particular faith. Nevertheless, library staff will need to be familiar with the social services offered by such groups in order to offer a fully functional relationship-based reference collection. This is where it's important to understand the full scope of services in terms of a continuum of care, which we explain later in this chapter. The ability to explain the role of a faith-based organization within the context of community services, along with the niche it fills, can provide a solid justification for why this "biased" source is part of the collection. In addition, many library staff members who don't know about larger social systems may be familiar with programs offered by churches, synagogues, and mosques in the community.

- **Other Nonprofit Agencies:** Small nonprofits can be key to connecting patrons with support services, but they're not always easy to find. One approach is to look for a county- or state-level association of nonprofits, which is similar in many ways to a business association. Another approach is to start by topic. For example, libraries that see a lot of need for services to immigrants can cast a net online and in person for new American support services. One great thing about a relationship-based approach is one solid connection can give entry into an existing network of organizations known to that person, eliminating the need for more traditional (and potentially less productive) research.

In the online resources, we include a list of these categories, along with some related websites. This can be used as a starting point for a library new to relationship-based reference or as a tool for libraries that have been building these relationships on the fly to identify and fill any gaps in their collection.

While it's helpful for one person to kick-start the project by creating an initial resource list, enabling all staff to understand what's in the "collection," even if they're not directly maintaining it, will help the library as a whole provide better service to patrons. A knowledgeable librarian who maintains a roster of agencies and understands what they offer can be a potential benefit to partners as well as patrons. Danelle described efforts she coordinated:

> It helped all of us at the library to feel better supported and to really be able to respond to people's needs and develop some resources that have been really helpful for us. One is a social service guide that is an ongoing collaboration between everyone in our branch and also the other branches of the library. . . . When people identify a useful service or resource in their neighborhood, they add it to that the guide, and it's all shared between us.

Her example highlights an important consideration, which is the collaborative nature of successful relationship-based resources.

The Living Relationship

Relationships, and thus a relationship-based reference collection, require attention and nourishment in order to thrive and grow. This means being present and having patience through many meetings and encounters that may not produce a "result" in the moment. Fahima, a librarian who has built a strong network of social service relationships in a small city, explains, "The library sits on a lot more community meetings than we ever have. So I sit in a homeless community network with all the agencies that are dealing with these issues. I find out about the issues, and then we also can offer, 'What can the library do? Here's resources we have, here is how we can collaborate.'" Sometimes relationships will take off right away, such as the one featured in chapter 2, where an initial meeting launched a lasting series of social service office hours in the library. Other times, relationship investments take years to pay off dividends. The main thing is to be there and be ready when the opportunity presents itself.

One way of understanding the role of libraries in the web of relationships is through a continuum of care model. Social workers see themselves embedded within larger social systems, rather than operating as individual organizations or entities, and a continuum of care reflects this.

Figure 1.1 can be used to map out any number of potential interactions in which librarians use their catalog of relationships to pass patrons to the appropriate next steps. In one simplified example, someone who comes to the library looking for supportive housing could be connected with a street outreach worker, who would then connect the patron to a housing case manager, and ideally, that patron finds stable housing and can return to the library with less urgent needs. In reality, successful passage through a continuum of care can take a lot of time, with people sometimes moving back and forth or falling all the way back to the beginning of the circle before

Figure 1.1

gaining enough traction to progress to the desired result. Still, the basic visual of the continuum is useful in that it shows how the library has a place in larger systems of care, so library staff don't have to feel responsible for ensuring the entire process functions well. Instead, they can focus on their piece of the whole, which is ensuring a personal handoff to known colleagues in organizations who can take on the next step in the process. The continuum also presents a useful visual of why the network of relationships, and not simply information, is so important to facilitate moving the patron/client from one organization to another.

One major challenge of a relationship-based reference collection is maintaining those relationships through a staff transition. Relationships can't be handed off from one person to another the way physical materials can. The ideal, whenever possible, is to involve more than one person in building the relationships. For example, Sara is paired with a Somali community liaison. While they don't do all the same day-to-day work, they both know and rely on many of the same community partners, so ultimately, when one of them leaves, the other can provide a bridge into those relationships for the new staff member. Libraries working with a smaller capacity could identify one primary librarian for relationship-building and give backup responsibilities to other, supporting staff members. Either way, managers will need to remember transitioning relationships takes time, plan ahead, and be prepared to have patience when one staff member leaves and a new one takes on the work of cultivating social service connections.

Social Work Concepts for Patron Services

Learning and applying basic social work concepts is a significant step libraries can take to improve patron service, even without a social worker on staff. This is where we provide the most training to library staff members, and it's where Sara began as a student who needed information on human services and found it in social work ideas. Taking a social work perspective on human behavior supports the purpose of a relationship-based reference collection and draws staff together into a common approach to challenging situations. Often, library staff members will start by asking how they can react to a situation: What are steps for conflict de-escalation? Whom do I call when a patron has a mental health breakdown? Those are important points to know, but they can be reactive in the moment, without addressing preparation and underlying issues. Much of what social workers can teach librarians comes from being proactive and not reactive with patrons—that is, taking the time and effort to foster empathy and humility in order to be prepared to manage challenging situations. Staff members who have a toolkit for understanding the different ways people move through the world are more welcoming to the community and also more resilient and less likely to burn out from work-related stress. Social work concepts and their utility in a library setting are embedded throughout this book. To lay the groundwork for them, we begin with a cornerstone concept for all social work: person-in-environment (PIE).

Person-in-Environment

PIE shines a light on everything in a person's life—including major life events, cultural currents, and personal traits—in order to reveal a complete and complex picture of who that person is. Human beings like to believe they have some control over their individual destinies, but through PIE, social workers are trained to consider both people and their environment as contributors to problems and solutions. The "environment" includes factors like their friends and family, the condition of their neighborhood, the quality of education they receive, the economy, the political environment, or even the way society views them. Assessing these, along with individual developmental, biological, cognitive, emotional, and physical attributes, is part of the process social workers use when trying to understand how to best help their clients. In short, PIE shapes the approach social workers use to analyze, describe, and assess human behavior.

Figure 1.2 shows that PIE draws upon the concepts of micro, mezzo, and macro practice mentioned earlier in this chapter. Social workers use these categories to parse out the many factors influencing a person's life. The intake assessments social workers complete with new clients are based on covering every possible aspect of these spheres of influence, and the list of things they address can be intimidating. We'll come back to this in chapter 4, where we talk about how social workers collect much more sensitive information as compared to librarians. For social workers, detailed information at every level creates a road map to the best interventions and services for the client, with the client providing additional explanations and expertise on their own experiences along the way. Understanding and using PIE is key to social work practice. It's also a great tool for librarians when it's applied with appreciation for the different boundaries libraries draw around private information and patron interactions.

In trainings, Sara is often asked whether understanding PIE means library staff should know all of these details about patrons. The answer, clearly, is no! What library staff can get from PIE is a lens to view patrons as whole persons. Rather than collecting details to design an intervention, the way social workers do, librarians can use PIE to understand more fully how little any of us know about each other in day-to-day life, how extensively those invisible factors may be influencing patron behavior, and thus why we should trust patrons to tell us who they are as experts on their own lives.

PIE SPHERES OF INFLUENCE

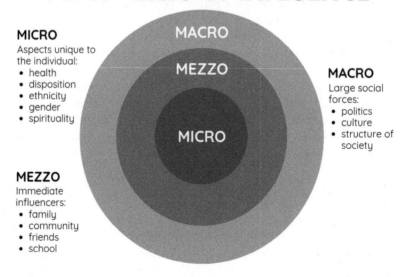

MICRO
Aspects unique to the individual:
- health
- disposition
- ethnicity
- gender
- spirituality

MEZZO
Immediate influencers:
- family
- community
- friends
- school

MACRO
Large social forces:
- politics
- culture
- structure of society

MACRO
MEZZO
MICRO

Figure 1.2

One example of how understanding the whole person creates empathy comes from Sara's experience in a branch library. Sara was the only librarian in the building, working off desk, when one of the support staff came to her and said, "There's a woman trying to use the scanner who's really angry. A few of us have tried to help her, but she's just not listening to instructions." So Sara ventured out into the library to see what was happening. She approached the lady at the computer with simple curiosity. What was she trying to do? What had she done so far? Rather than expect hostility based on what other staff members had said (and these were trustworthy colleagues sharing their own genuine experience of the patron), Sara chose to take the patron's perspective and accept what she heard. It became clear pretty quickly that the patron was trying to accomplish something a single-page scanner wasn't meant to do, and indeed she didn't seem to hear or process any instructions or explanation. But in the safety of being listened to for her experience rather than focusing on the task at hand, the patron disclosed she was dealing with a personal tragedy and was on a tight deadline to leave town and deal with it. Sara didn't need this detail in order to be empathetic—she assumed there was some unknown factor in the patron's behavior that was larger than her frustration with library staff. But by revealing that detail, the patron confirmed the validity of a whole person approach. She was so flooded with emotion that she had no space to take in anything else, which is a genuine psychological state anyone may enter under high levels of stress. Ultimately, Sara wasn't able to help the patron get her scanning done before she left, but she did give the patron a chance to be received with respect. By understanding PIE before entering that situation, Sara also created a space within herself where she knew the patron's behavior wasn't meant as a personal attack and could let it go when she left work.

Sara's experience also demonstrates the use of trauma-informed care (TIC) in a library setting. TIC has become a popular training topic for frontline staff, with Denver Public Library's lead social worker, Elissa Hardy, often stepping up at the national level to talk about its importance in libraries. In their first-ever collective, public statement, a group of the major urban library social workers and their library directors chose to highlight TIC as a core service they provide, saying, "We work extensively with library staffers to help them better understand the effects of trauma and how to minimize triggering behavior when interacting with customers. We help staff members understand their own strengths and how they can utilize their own experiences to better serve customers" (Jeske et al. 2018). TIC uses the PIE approach of recognizing the impact of major life events on an individual's reality and applies it specifically to trauma, often focusing on adverse childhood experiences, or ACEs. We include a few leads into the wealth of information and training available about TIC and ACEs in this chapter's online resources, and we support its application in libraries. We also want to emphasize TIC is just one "slice of PIE." Every person is greater than the trauma they experienced, and libraries benefit from the positive influences patrons bring as whole people, as well as having the chance to respond with empathy to challenges arising from negative experiences.

One caveat to keep in mind with TIC and PIE is we use them to understand and explain behavior, not to predict behavior. When used as a predictor, lessons learned from PIE can lead to dangerous stereotyping. One way we've heard of this information being misused is: People experiencing homelessness come primarily from impoverished backgrounds. People who grow up in poverty hear fewer words in their early life than folks who are more well-off, so they have smaller vocabularies. Therefore, when you're talking to homeless patrons, you should simplify your language to meet them at their level. This is exactly what we don't want to do with PIE. There's actual science referenced in this example: a famous study recorded and counted the number of words heard by young children from different economic backgrounds and demonstrated a deficit among children living in poverty (Fernald, Marchman, and Weisleder 2013). But the way we want to use this information is not to assume patrons experiencing homelessness, or for that matter anyone living in poverty, will have a small vocabulary (not to mention some library staff members themselves may have grown up in poverty!). Instead, this information gives us a reason to offer respect to anyone who struggles to communicate because we understand that far from being "stupid," they might not have had the same advantages in life as someone with a wider range of expression.

PIE in Action

Appendix A is a blank PIE chart worksheet to print and use. You can also download a larger version in the online resources. We often recommend starting by completing a PIE chart for yourself as an individual. Not only is this a good way to get a sense of the meaning of the different spheres of influence, but it can also be a significant tool for self-knowledge. Being able to define and name your own influencers is the first step in self-awareness for identifying and managing personal biases. The PIE chart can also be a starting place for understanding and exploring the needs of a particular population the library wants to serve better, an assessment of whether a particular library program is responding to community needs, or just about any use you can devise. Figure 1.3 illustrates a sample PIE chart and how it might incorporate some typical programs and community engagement provided by libraries into the spheres of influence.

Often, when libraries address one or two challenges, they may feel they've fixed the problem and then wonder why they're still not getting the attendance or reaching the audience they expect. Sara recently had an

PIE LEVELS OF INTERVENTION

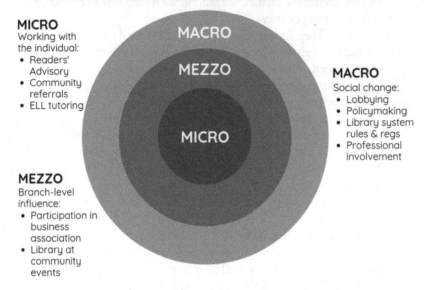

MICRO
Working with
the individual:
- Readers'
  Advisory
- Community
  referrals
- ELL tutoring

MEZZO
Branch-level
influence:
- Participation in
  business
  association
- Library at
  community
  events

MACRO
Social change:
- Lobbying
- Policymaking
- Library system
  rules & regs
- Professional
  involvement

Figure 1.3

experience that gave her insight into how PIE can help. While researching refugee mental health, she came across an article that included the results of focus groups from several communities in Minneapolis and St. Paul, including one in the neighborhood she serves through the public library. The reasons participants gave for why they don't seek mental health treatment included elements at every level of PIE: personal shame, especially from men who felt the need to appear strong (micro); family pressure not to do anything that would jeopardize a much-needed job (mezzo); and a cultural concept of "craziness" that never evolved to include language or space for "mental health" (macro) (Shannon et al. 2015). While she wasn't about to design a mental health program, Sara did recognize many of the factors in the article as the same or similar to barriers she had witnessed to the success of other library programs, leading to the idea of using PIE as a tool for identifying and addressing barriers in a holistic way. Her hope is that by mapping needs to this standard model, she can better demonstrate why it's in the scope of library services to address patron challenges at many levels in order for programs to truly succeed. She is interested in continuing to experiment with this approach and hopes to hear from practitioners who test it in their own work.

Online Resources

www.wholepersonlibrarianship.com/book/resources/chapter1

- Quick guide to potential partners with agency links
- Printable PIE worksheet
- Links to:
  - Trauma-informed care resources
  - CROC website
- Additional resources provided by you and your colleagues

CHAPTER TWO

Partners in the Library

Some of these social service agencies who have social workers or mental health providers, they don't have a place to land. Their school space is at a premium. If you could only find some of these folks would like to co-locate with you in the beginning, form a partnership on site and then little by little see if they'd be able to offer a couple hours a day. I just know administrators are going to say, "a $60,000 position—I don't have the money for a full-time social worker." People put up the barriers right away, but if you could look at having those interviews, getting folks to come to your library, offering a little space for them to meet folks for their own work, and then see if a partnership can develop. That might be a way to get them in the door.

—Georgia, social worker

Overview

This chapter details several paths to hosting professional social workers and social service providers in libraries. This is a frequent starting point for libraries, and many find it meets their patrons' needs without having to hire a social worker to staff. Both public and academic libraries may find this model useful because it can be adapted to incorporate community partners as well as student services. It's a low-cost or completely free option that works well for small budgets, and it doesn't require the same supervisory time investment as hosting an intern. It's worth noting, too, that many of the basic concerns about patron needs and library capacity we explore in this chapter also apply to services provided by social work interns, so reviewing this content is a good stepping stone if it's the direction you plan to take.

The chapter begins with an example of a successful and long-running partnership between a suburban library system and social services, aimed at patrons experiencing homelessness. We then move on to discuss how to start these collaborations and some of the elements to consider in such partnerships. We offer examples of the types of partnerships you can consider and conclude with suggestions for documenting participation and collecting participant feedback as a foundation for hiring a social worker, if your library decides to take that step.

Harrison's Story

Harrison, a circulation manager in a suburban library, started to observe some changes in the community members who visited his library following the economic downturn in 2008. Many regular library patrons lined up before the library opened each day, and they'd often stay for hours, if not all day. Most looked like anyone else—they were relatively clean and well attired—but they spent an unusual amount of time asking to use the service desk phones or tidying up in the bathrooms. Others, who had bags and carts, started hanging out in front of the library fireplace. Staff noticed a tent encampment go up on the south side of the library. Tensions rose in the library café because patrons requested free condiments and ice water without buying food. Harrison said,

> We had very definite examples of homeless persons living right on the library property. Wetlands and groves of trees provided some cover on the backside of the library, and there was an accessible, inviting open sheltered area beneath our public deck. In addition, you could see cars beginning to use our parking lot overnight. In the morning, the inhabitants of the cars would be outside the main entrance, alongside other folks with grocery carts, standing or sitting around a half hour before opening, waiting for us to open the doors. Many of these folks hung out all day right up until closing time at our branch.

These were all classic signs his patrons were experiencing housing insecurity, but the final straw for Harrison was the report of a woman found dead in a ditch just blocks from the library. There were no signs of foul play. Her description closely matched that of a regular patron who had suddenly stopped coming to the library. In a brief exchange with her prior to her disappearance, Harrison learned the patron was a recent transplant who had fallen on hard times. He said, "She would come in early and stay all day, every day. The article described her as an ex-teacher from the West Coast with a history of mental health issues. Without being 100% certain this person was the same one found within walking distance of the library, there was a haunting feeling that someone in our midst that needed help [and] didn't get it." Harrison felt certain her death was connected to her housing status, and the library could have done something for her if it had resources at hand for someone in her situation.

Harrison already had some idea of how to support his patrons in need, but when he learned about library-social work collaborations at his state library association's annual conference, he knew he wanted to implement one in his library. He reflected, "I remember coming out from that session and having these idealist talks with a couple other librarian friends on the banks overlooking the river and thinking, 'Yeah, I would really love to do this.' I was a social work major in college, and this seemed like another aspect of working in libraries that really fit my interests." Eventually, he mentioned the idea to Georgia, a social worker and director of a county social services collaborative, who was so excited about the idea she volunteered to organize a meeting of local social service providers. He laughed as he recalled, "And I just mentioned to her that I had been seeing some stuff in our library and I had been thinking about doing a social work program. And she's like, 'Oh that's great. Do you want me to help you organize a meeting?' It was right on the spur of the moment. I hadn't really expected to be taken seriously, but Georgia took it seriously. And I said, 'Sure, okay.'"

That initial meeting was attended by over 20 different providers from a diverse group of community organizations and government agencies. This included two school districts; the library; county social services, including child protection, mental health, housing, and the department of health; the police department; city representatives; the YMCA; the Salvation Army; a homeless shelter; a domestic violence shelter; churches; a food shelf; and local nonprofits providing human services.

The conversation focused on the growing homelessness the organizations observed in this first-ring suburb. The area lacked a shelter, which was a barrier for citizens who needed immediate access to housing. Harrison commented, "First-ring suburban homelessness . . . is a little bit off of the chart because there are not as many organizations tracking and reaching the people that are in those areas, and in many respects, people in those areas are fleeing the city for safety reasons, and they want to be hidden as much as they can be. In other respects, they want help but don't know how to find it in those areas." Harrison's community isn't alone in facing this sort of challenge. According to the Department of Housing and Urban Development, nearly 50% of people experiencing homelessness live in areas outside of major cities (Henry et al. 2018), but many people don't realize suburban and rural homelessness can look different from how it appears in urban settings.

At that meeting, a core group of service providers quickly agreed to form a pilot collaboration at the library. The collaboration was modeled after a similar program a local nonprofit was hosting in the downtown library of a nearby urban system. One of the initial social workers to participate, Iris, worked for a human service organization and volunteered her time in the library. She said, "The idea was a couple times a month we would go and spend an hour in the library, different social workers every time but familiar faces, and the same ones were back every month, and we would just touch base with the patrons in the library that needed some extra support and basic needs. It was not just those experiencing homelessness but those needing help with health insurance or finding clothing resources or food and things like that, some transportation needs." All of the meeting participants agreed to spread the word and distribute flyers developed by members of the group. The library made an extra effort to reach patrons by putting small flyers about the program at each computer terminal and by offering coffee and snacks as an incentive for folks to show up.

The program started holding "office hours" at the library less than three months after the initial partner meeting. At the first session, five patrons arrived in need of assistance with housing, disability services, and health care access. By week three, patron demand meant the library needed to extend the office hour to an hour and a half. Within three months, the director of the library system asked Harrison to expand the program to another branch. In the initial six months of the original program, over 100 adults were served, a count not including the many children who benefitted from access to early childhood programs; childcare assistance; and the food, cash, housing, immigration, and mental health services provided to their parents. In the ensuing years, these numbers have continued to increase, and the program regularly serves over 75 adult patrons per quarter.

One potential challenge Harrison has faced is rapid turnover among staff from the library's partnering agencies. Nonprofit staff members, in particular, frequently switch jobs, making continuity an ongoing concern. Fortunately, the organizations involved have seen enough benefit to remain committed through change and keep up their participation. One large nonprofit in the area has been exceptionally dedicated, as it has essentially anchored the program at both sites for its entire run. Recruiting new, supplemental partners from time to time can fine tune the array of services on offer, such as when a senior services organization agreed to provide a social worker once a month to work with aging patrons who were looking for assistance.

Another challenge the program faced after its launch was the development of what Harrison described as a "dual culture" space, where patrons come not only for help from social service providers but also to experience a "kind of drop in center for homeless folks looking for connection [and] check-ins, as well as the free coffee and snacks." Offering these services required a visible and spacious room, which at the original site was addressed by reserving the board room each Tuesday afternoon for several hours. At the second site, the only available space was smaller and less visible, so it worked well for consultations but wasn't as effective as a drop-in center. Harrison suggests anyone planning this kind of program should "pay attention to the space you are going to offer. And how you are going to use that space. Issues like confidentiality can arise in a smaller space. In a larger space, you might cultivate that drop-in vibe a little more. People might have a little more elbow room and feel a little more comfortable coming back. . . . That relationship in the library space is a big piece of making success for that individual possible because they can be more comfortable there."

Harrison would love to expand the program by asking social service providers to spend more time in the library or even have a dedicated county social worker operating exclusively out of the library. At the moment, however, the current program doesn't require much in the way of financial resources or library staff time, which matches the library's current capacity to provide support. The social workers who come to the library do so on a pro-bono basis or as part of their duties within their specific organization. Having one partner in particular to anchor the program each week at both sites, then supplementing with additional partners once or twice a month, has worked very well. Snacks, supplies such as care kits, and printing are all donated by the involved organizations. Because the libraries are financed primarily through county funding, a next step could be enlisting the help of key players on the county board, something Harrison hopes to accomplish in future years.

In reflecting on the program, which at the time of the interview was three years old, Harrison said, "What we set out to do has definitely been a success, a sustained success. And by success, I mean I think we really have met a need that was in that specific community and continues to be in that community."

Inspiration into Justification

Harrison's initiative was sparked by his experiences with one patron and the knowledge the library could do more for people like her. One or two highly motivated staff members can be the catalyst for this kind of change, driven by personal experience and observation in the library. Sometimes, as in the case of Elana, a whole person approach comes from connections outside of work: "As a librarian who was married to a clinical social worker, I have very specific ideas about what we need to do. . . . I really feel like I had the best [of] both worlds because I came to understand the scope of what my husband did in helping families through all kinds of amazing things. . . . There is a role for libraries, and that's what excites me about what we're taking on, there's a need." As a library director, Elana has been able to divert some of her library's financial resources to helping patrons experiencing homelessness, and she's been able to demonstrate real action in areas where other government agencies have stalled in connecting people with services.

In other cases, library staff may find inspiration more gradually, through the accumulation of many smaller interactions over time. Jakeem, a library administrator in a large suburban area, shared how his patrons prompted him to think about providing social services: "The type of questions [patrons] asked organically led me to believe that there was a different type of conversation that needed to be taking place for some of the patrons than we could offer at our public service desk." Jakeem shared his reference desk observations with other library staff: "And that's kind of the way I pitched the program in the beginning to people who were skeptical, was [that] these types of information needs or requests are happening anyway. It's not like a new program per se. I mean, the demand is already there. It's just bringing in the right person." He ultimately created a successful partnership to host social work office hours in the library.

While personal stories can provide significant motivation for change, other people's experiences do need to be handled with care. Harrison's story about the woman who passed away can be included here because her obituary made her situation into publicly available information. In other instances, including some of the interviews for this book, patrons' stories needed to be withheld in order to respect the sanctity of their privacy and autonomy. This is part of the social work values of "dignity and worth of the person" and trusting people as experts on their own lives. As we'll discuss further in chapter 4, social workers collect much more sensitive information than librarians do, but they also take tremendous care to protect what they learn. In that respect, Jakeem's observations have the advantage of being easier to quantify and anonymize across multiple patron experiences. However, Harrison's experience also provides an example of how to use a single interaction to see the community in a new way and begin to collect those more universal observations. He started to take note of changes in the library, using clear, judgment-free language: patrons were spending more time at the library, brought more possessions with them, and used their time differently than in the past, among other behaviors. He also saw changes in the neighborhood, including tent encampments and lived-in cars. These observations culminated in his being ready when he met a like-minded social worker. He may not have had to provide formal justification up front, but he had knowledge of patron needs and social service models he could connect directly to the organizations Georgia invited to the table.

One caution to keep in mind while working with personal observations is not all challenges are visible in public, and not everyone who is experiencing some kind of crisis will look the way you expect them to look. An outreach manager at a large, urban public library made sure to mention this in her recommendations to others who do this work:

> [Our outreach worker] often walks around the building and introduces herself to groups the folks, and . . . even though she has sort of a lengthy background in social services, she's been really surprised by the fact that she's often gone up to groups of folks and given her spiel thinking none of these folks are going to be my demographic, just based on appearances, and she's been really surprised to discover that it's very, very often the folks that she assumed would not need social services who do end up stopping by her drop-ins. So, I [recommend] just thinking about ways to broaden the scope and not stereotype folks based on their appearance because it's really impossible to tell who is in need of services and who isn't.

Harrison was aware of this more in hindsight, as he looked back at the woman who passed away as "reasonably well taken care of and dressed." This doesn't mean you should disregard the obvious needs, but rather offers a reminder to contemplate what may be invisible but still ultimately require attention.

Harrison had already been thinking about how to address homelessness in his library's community, but the observations leading to library-social work collaboration can be related to any number of social service issues. Other common concerns addressed by social workers in libraries include hunger, poverty, mental health, substance abuse, and personal crisis management. This is where spending some time on the concepts in chapter 1 can be helpful before initiating a partnership, even for libraries that are eager to take one on. Building a relationship-based reference collection and understanding the library community and its resources from a PIE perspective can help the library determine and define specific community needs, which is important to know before approaching partners for assistance. Libraries may also start by deciding to perform a community needs assessment, a specialty of social workers that can be a good task for a social work intern (see chapter 3). For libraries wanting to conduct their own needs assessment, we provide a comprehensive list of example questions in appendix B and online. This is the same handout Mary gives to her beginning social work students. This sample needs assessment is meant to provide a buffet of options, from which a library should choose just a handful based on the direction it wants to take. Also, as the preceding examples demonstrate, formal assessment is completely optional at this point. Some administrators and decision makers may want that kind of information up front, but for most folks, jumping into service first and then assessing the results is sufficient.

Justification into Action

So, who is the "right person" or people to address the needs of your patrons? If you've been spending time in the community, connecting with partners, and understanding the services they offer and the gaps waiting to be filled, it should be relatively straightforward to take the next step of matching those partners to your particular patron needs. If the library looking for social service partners has some autonomy to make this decision without first seeking bureaucratic approval, this could be as simple as listing a few of the needs observed among patrons, then brainstorming one or two community partners who could potentially address them. But librarians who don't already have a fulsome understanding of their community partners—those who are new on the job or need to get something started quickly—have plenty of options. One relatively simple place to start is the PIE chart from chapter 1, which can be used at two levels: first, to brainstorm the potential needs and influencers of a particular patron population, and then to determine which community partners exist to address those needs at each level. Staff can also replicate what Harrison and Georgia did by bringing together a group of agencies who work on the same issues. People who work at those agencies are already familiar with community needs and can articulate quickly what would be helpful to them. In fact, as Iris recalled, "Social workers are already there. . . . I met a lot of my regular caseload clients in libraries as I didn't have a regular place to meet with them, and my office was not a confidential space. So, I was either making home visits, or we were meeting out in the community, a lot of times at libraries." The group of partners assembled by the library could help design a PIE-based response together, or if the library is already familiar with its patron needs, it can present those and see how they align with partner needs. Either way, key things to keep in mind are (1) a partnership should have benefits to each organization involved, and (2) a clear definition of what the library and partners hope to accomplish is a good first step toward ensuring everyone's needs are being met.

As you work to identify your library and community needs, some other questions to ask include:

- What are you ready to commit to doing?
- What are others ready to do?
- Who are your patrons?
- What are your patron needs?
- Will patrons be involved, and if so, how will they be involved?
- What is your library's financial situation and priorities?
- What would be a good starting point for you?
- What kind of personal and professional support and resources do you have?

- What kind of opposition might you encounter?
- Are there unlikely allies/champions you can invite to the conversation?

Types of Partnerships

Some library-social service partnerships happen with solo organizations, and some involve groups. Harrison and Georgia assembled a diverse group of partners, but other public libraries have crafted different arrangements to suit their needs. Some have focused on housing, some on behavioral health, some on yet other issues. There are as many paths to success as there are patron needs in your community. Here are some examples of the types of partnerships happening in libraries across the United States:

- **Single partner with one or more outreach workers:**
  - "We actually partnered with . . . a nonprofit that tries to get people housing, whether it is temporary or permanent. About four years ago, we began a partnership with them where we have [some of their staff] called navigators. They are not trained social workers, but they are embedded in our library, and the most recent navigator is the most successful one. He is a former minister who has gone through some issues himself, and he spent every day in the library trying to find housing, clothing, and resources for these people who are definitely at-risk." —Elana, urban library director
  - "We got a grant . . . and we have a behavioral specialist that we hire through an independent contractor, and she provides open office hours for families, individuals, and couples."—Lily, library branch manager
  - "We started it from basically scratch with a very limited amount of money. It grew to the point where we had pretty successful outcomes and collaboration with the police department that seemed to generate a lot of positive experience about it. The basic design about the program was that it is was appointment-based, one-on-one intake, interview, and referral session that happened in the library. [Then] the folks were referred out or helped to other agencies in that city."—Jakeem, library administrator
- **Combined model (embedded partner with supplementary additional organization visits):**
  - "Part of what I do is I supervise our community resource specialist project, which is a partnership that we have with the largest shelter here . . . and homeless services organizations to have a staff person at our library who's offering social service information and referral. I also coordinate a lot of other social service agencies being in our building, providing community resources and referral to our patrons, like . . .

I organize the free tax help with United Way and things like that."
—Kai, urban librarian

- **Multiple partners coalescing around a shared issue:**

  - "[Our organization covered] really mainly the basic needs as far as food and housing. Others did a little bit more of the transportation and help for adults staying outside completely unsheltered. And then there was food shelf folks, too, who were there to provide those resources, and we had some domestic violence [service] providers. It was a really good mix of people, and we got the same people showing up at the same times each month."—Iris, social worker

  - "In the last three or four years we've developed a wellness corner, where we invited lots of different agencies from our community to bring their expertise to us. So, we have a mental health worker and social workers come in a couple times a week, we have nursing students that do practicums in public health here six months out of the year in administering noninvasive health screenings, have dietitians and physical therapists that give informational sessions, just a whole variety of different programs. We're bringing the human formats instead of a DVD to the public and serve about 200 homeless in the community"—Mai, librarian

  - "We have something called community coffee hour on Friday mornings, and we started that shortly after the election. Whenever tensions were high, the atmosphere was very charged here in the library. So we thought we'd open up Friday mornings with some coffee and some conversation, and there we've gotten to meet people in another context. We bring in different service providers, not to do a presentation or anything like that but chat and get out their business cards and information, and we found that that's been a really wonderful way to connect people and social service providers."—Nikita, librarian

Of all of the collaborations listed here, Nikita's program of sharing coffee and discussion has become the most popular. Started at the Dallas Public Library (DPL) in 2013 (Dallas Library 2014), this model has since been replicated across North America, including at the libraries featured in example stories in chapters 3, 5, and 6. Coffee & Conversation, as it's known in the official DPL model, fosters relationship-building between library staff and patrons, giving them a place to connect as peers outside of the traditional desk interaction. Just like it sounds, it centers activities around people talking and having coffee (and sometimes snacks) together, with the key piece being inclusion of staff in the activity and not just as planners. By focusing on building relationships with partners, this program creates a framework for having more positive interactions around challenging issues in the future, and it also creates a regular gathering space that doesn't necessarily always have to include a social service partner. Sometimes, the program can be used for games or crafts, while other days may offer a place for social service organizations to test out what could become a more lasting partnership. A quick guide to bringing Coffee & Conversation to any library is available through the Programming Librarian website and is included in this chapter's online resources.

Action into Sustainability

A crucial element to any partnership, and one that is often out of individual control, is wholehearted buy-in from all partners. Harrison and Georgia had great luck to have found each other when they did, and Georgia was immediately invested in the idea of being present in the library. Not everyone will have the same level of serendipity, and sometimes organizations will make an initial agreement but need ongoing proof the partnership is worth their time and energy. Iris explained her own experience with this at the start of a collaboration: "It was a little difficult to get our organizations to agree to let us come there for the hour or a couple hours each month, just because we had so many other things going on, and our primary commitments were to our primary clients, so with our caseload to do that hour of outreach was a bit of a stretch." We already touched on the fact that it's important to consider how the collaboration can meet both library and partner needs. There are two additional factors to consider in order to continue to meet those needs and maintain a sustainable collaboration.

Space in the Library

As we saw with Harrison, functional space in the library matters to sustainable collaboration and the types of activities that succeed within it. In addition to thinking about traffic flow, it's important to consider issues of patron access, privacy, and confidentiality. As Kai, a librarian involved in collaboration, noted, "A lot of these social services interviews are very sensitive [in order for providers] to understand what folks are qualified for, but our library buildings are not really built with that kind of privacy plus safety in mind." She also raised the issue of safety for an isolated social service provider:

> We really struggled and have tried a lot of different things in terms of finding a balance between keeping [the service provider] safe and protecting the privacy of patrons. We're hoping that in the remodel that's going to happen in some areas of our central library next year . . . that's one of the problems we'll be able to solve.

Of course, remodeling isn't a quick fix or even near-term option for many libraries, and existing spaces may not be ideal. Library staff can walk through placement options with the service provider(s) and regularly check in on how it's working, not only to make the service as functional as possible but also to show respect for the partner's expertise and needs. Everyone involved in the collaboration should approach library spaces with an open mind and a willingness to balance services with the limits of what's available.

Data Collection and Sharing

Keeping track of and sharing data is helpful when launching a program and essential to justifying continued staff time for both library staff and social service providers. Data might be research on best practices, community observations, contacts with partners, resources, challenges, your own experiences, and the stories of your patrons. As Georgia shared, sometimes data collection is the impetus for moving partnerships forward: "I think sometimes you don't wait for the administrators to move forward. What you do is you show research that this is the best practice, then you reach out to your local mental health providers, your school folks, your folks who work with chronically homeless folks. You get them together in a room, and you say, hey, how can we do some outreach together?"

Librarians are fortunate that their social service partners are usually required to keep detailed records of all their client interactions, so there may be no need to invent a whole new tracking model. However, as we mentioned in the introduction, librarians and social workers do have some potential ethical conflicts in the types of data they collect and store, as well as how they approach sharing information. It's worth having a conversation at the start of any partnership to find out what data each social service partner needs to collect, what the library would like to harvest from or add to it, and how it will be shared. Usually, partnerships only require some basic information collection by the library; we delve into a more detailed discussion of collaborative data collection and sharing in chapter 4.

Benefits to Community Partners

In addition to inspirational stories and data-sharing, libraries offer a laundry list of benefits to social service partners. These can make excellent talking points but can also become more meaningful to partners once they have direct experience in the library. It's always useful to name and highlight benefits over time as a support to sustainability as well as an initial impetus for collaboration. Some of the perks of library-social work collaboration mentioned in our focus groups include:

- **Library as Safe Space:** "We've become incredibly popular with the other agencies because we're a central location. We're easy to get to. We're neutral—there is a lot of stigma attached to going out to social services, whereas everybody can come [to the library].”—Mai, librarian

- **Library as First Point of Contact:** “By far the most successful outcomes we were having were with people who had slipped through the cracks in some way but weren't immediately presenting themselves to [social service or library] staff or to the community, for example, as homeless or as having an acute mental illness.”—Jakeem, library administrator

- **Library as Freedom to Meet People Where They Are:** “When we would put together programming on social services that are available or a workshop on applying for housing, there wasn't very much attendance, and some of the people that most were interested in that were in library at the time. They were really attracted to, really interested in the possibility in a one-on-one conversation with me and sitting down and not having to glean through lots and lots of information and pull out what specifically was useful to them.”—Nikita, librarian

- **Library as Fellow Public Entity:** “In our case because we're . . . a county-driven social services system, and we are a county library, [that means] we are a department within the county just as social services are. . . . I think you have some social services directors that could see that is a major opportunity as outreach, as an outpost for their workers to be a little bit more involved with the clients that they serve.”—Owen, librarian

- **Library as a Site of Social Service Cross-Pollination:** “Social workers don't have a lot of time at their disposal, so that's why they actually volunteer their time to work collaboratively with the library one day a week—they found that they benefit from that cross-fertilization of resource knowledge. We have some folks that are working with chronically mentally ill folks, some folks that work on homelessness, some with veterans, some with young children, some are school folks, so the interdisciplinary piece is an advantage to all the practitioners. They grow together and learn together.”—Georgia, social worker

Unfortunately, it's still sometimes the case that the best stories and justification in the world can't engage someone who is too busy or doesn't have the perspective to understand a library-social work partnership. It can also be challenging to bring together multiple partners at the same time—busy schedules are difficult to align. Library staff should prepare for roadblocks and participant turnover on the journey to success and be willing to keep trying. If an initial attempt to bring people together doesn't succeed, there's no need to be discouraged. Set aside time for further relationship-building. Focus on observed community needs and how those align to the missions of potential partner organizations. When a partner does take some time to be available in the library, document every collectible piece of information from those interactions to bring to other potential partners. Success ultimately can depend on patience, commitment, and the willingness to start small and build incrementally. As Georgia said, "The only barrier really is [the service providers] did find it takes a while for the library patrons to get to know who they are and what they're about. But as it takes off, there doesn't seem to be any barrier. Folks do benefit from that cross-fertilization, and then they bring all that knowledge back to their own jobs, and it seems to be working out really well."

Adaptations for Academic Libraries

Academic libraries, and community college libraries in particular, have also been growing their involvement in social service partnerships. In fact, the first peer-reviewed conference paper offering research on library-social work collaboration was written by a community college library director and explored the role of academic libraries in connecting students to social services. As the author of that paper acknowledged, even in 2015, which was before the largest uptick in public library-social work partnerships, growth was slower in academic libraries (Hines 2015). However, the need for services in many academic libraries is very real. Academic librarians most often find success with their own relationship-based reference collection and with this chapter's "office hours in the library" model of service, both of which can be adapted to include campus resources alongside community resources, depending on the size and scope of the college or university that is the library's home.

Academic librarians have been observing and responding to trends that are borne out by statistics about students. The archetypal undergraduate, who heads to college just out of high school and finishes their degree in four or five years with the help of family and financial aid, may be more prevalent at elite schools, but they're not the overwhelming majority overall. For example, 33% of undergraduate students have an income below $20,000 per year, and of those, two out of three support themselves independently (NCES 2018). Working in a community college library, Pilar saw the effects of low income on students: "I've had students disclose to me that they're going to be evicted and they don't have housing; that they're going to have to drop out because they don't have childcare; I've had students tell me they have to decide between buying books and buying food. A lot of situations like that, I think, 'There's a solution for this. Let me help you find some information on how to connect with these services.'"

Students in four-year institutions experience these issues, too. Quincy, who works at a large university library, said, "At our location we started a food shelf for our student workers that were experiencing food insecurity. We do a lot with learning support across the spectrum—the libraries a structural level are trying to work with the university to get some unification across that and consistency and make it easier to navigate." Both Pilar and Quincy saw their interactions with students as a natural extension of their work: Pilar through her relationship-based reference collection and Quincy through a micro-level intervention (food shelf) and macro-level efforts to connect disparate campus resources.

Librarians also learn of student mental health issues during reference consultations. Ryanne, a social work librarian, saw burnout in those students:

> We start out one-on-one discussing their research interests or their research questions, and because I feel like I can create a pretty safe environment to let them explore what their questions are, it's happened a handful of times where it turns into—they just disclose more about what's going on in their day-to-day life or even in their past and how it connects to what got them into the social work profession. I know that I think I could speak for [my colleague], she won't mind me saying this there was one time where she actually had to walk a student up to the mental health services, to the student services, because it was clear to her that was no longer a reference consultation, that the student needed outside services.

This reflects a growing trend of documented mental health concerns in both undergraduate and graduate students (e.g., Supiano 2018). Sasha, an academic medical school librarian, shared how she established a partnership with student mental health services: "If there's anything that exceeds our capacity, if we notice a student with particular challenges or a problematic student, we can refer to them [to the behavioral response team]. They've been fantastic, and they're pretty good about coming to the library at the beginning of semester and clarifying what their services are. So I feel like we can work with them pretty easily." Framing the library as an entry point for existing campus resources can be one way to address growing concerns about how schools support the whole-student experience.

Despite these successful examples, it's relatively common for academic librarians to face administrative resistance to efforts that would take library staff time away from existing services. Hines (2015) speculates a "potential factor for the decreased outreach and awareness of these issues among libraries in higher education [as compared to public libraries] could be because most institutions of higher education already provide outreach and awareness but through other outlets; i.e., campus health centers or financial aid offices." To put it more bluntly, student needs that aren't strictly information-based haven't been part of the traditional academic library experience, and many administrators (and librarian colleagues) will still see relationship-based services as outside the scope of their library's mission. Pilar shared how she ran into these restrictions when she changed jobs: "I've been sort of siloed, which upsets me coming in because I had done a lot of research at my previous institution and a lot of groundwork [to establish services in the library], and in here there's a lot of 'No, that's student services' job, don't touch it.'"

Making the case for student or social services in the library, and for library staff time spent building those relationships, is possible with additional prep work to fit the services into a library context. Sasha explained, "If you can make a case within academia as to where librarians can fit in with various professionals as to how they support [students] in terms of gathering knowledge, gathering information, that might be a direction that libraries could go toward. Particularly if you're in social work, you have to know a lot about the community resources, and so I think and that can play into a major piece about collaboration." This is a helpful context for first-year experience librarians as well as those who support social services departments: part of the whole-student college experience is building knowledge of their new community, and that's something librarians can incorporate into an information framework.

In libraries with robust student services and many students living on campus, it can be relatively straightforward to bridge student needs revealed during library interactions and the resources that stand ready to address them, but schools with reduced student services and large numbers of commuter students face greater challenges. Approximately 40% of low-income students choose two-year schools, and the more income students have, the more likely they are to choose a four-year school (NCES 2018). Meanwhile, two-year schools are less likely to provide extensive student support services. Add to that fact that low-income students are more likely to use the library for reliable internet connections and full-service computer use, and not only will community college librarians see more students with the need for support in their daily lives, they're also less able to refer them to immediate, on-campus assistance. Pilar addressed this in her library by adapting a solution that was pioneered in a dual-use, academic-public library:

> I used some information I got from San Jose State University for their program, which is what I modeled it on, which helped set forth good ground rules. . . . I had worked with the school of social work to set up an internship program within the community college library, where folks could sign up for a 20 minute appointment focused on practical needs like food, food assistance, help finding childcare, or help with housing and reach some sort of connections that way. . . . [Bringing] in people that were in the social work department as opposed to doing it ourselves helped a lot to address the concerns that we had.

She was also able to help build justification through the fact that the library was one of the few places on campus able to offer appropriate meeting space:

"Being able to provide the space was a large part of why our idea of having the social workers come into the library was accepted by our administration. . . . We had a private meeting space if we used our study rooms for the few hours a week." Chapter 3 may be useful to those who want to attempt Pilar's model and also includes some information on more traditional library services specifically for social work students.

There remains a great deal of work to be done in academic libraries, by academic librarians, to determine whether this will become a justified and sustainable movement, and whether it will be implemented across all types of libraries or only those serving students with the greatest need. We're seeing a rapid increase in interest from reference and instruction librarians and from circulation desk supervisors in our trainings on this topic, and we look forward to working with colleagues at academic libraries as they expand their definition of information services.

Online Resources

www.wholepersonlibrarianship.com/book/resources/chapter2

- Links for academic librarians to research on student demographics and mental health
- Customizable and printable version of the community needs assessment (also see appendix B)
- Programming Librarian information on starting Coffee & Conversation
- Additional resources provided by you and your colleagues

CHAPTER THREE

Social Work Students: "Living the Dream" in the Library

Social work today, [being in libraries] is kind of the dream. . . . We literally get to meet people where they're at, and I love that. They don't have to come to me, I can just come to them. And I really love the opportunity to be able to provide services in that way.

—*Tyra, library social worker*

Overview

In this chapter, we will explain the basics of social work education and how to find and supervise a social work intern in your library. Social work professors and internship directors may also find this chapter useful for understanding some of the needs of libraries and how to connect to them as placement sites.

Social work internships in libraries can provide a wealth of benefits. Many libraries that now have full-time social workers started out with a social work intern as a way to test and document need. These arrangements also open a whole new world of internship sites for schools of social work, which are always looking for appropriate placements. These close working relationships foster better understanding between librarianship and social work of the ways we function as sister professions, and by extension they provide a clearer picture of the whole lives of our patrons.

We start this chapter with the example of an exceptionally successful social work internship at a library, which has blossomed into lasting employment and new opportunities. We then explore the fundamentals of social work education and internship placement as they relate to libraries and provide some sample documents both libraries and social work internship coordinators can use to get started. The chapter continues with a review of the unique benefits and challenges of hosting a social work intern, then closes with some additional examples of internships.

Jason's Story

Jason Pearl[1] started as an MSW intern at Kansas City Public Library (KCPL), where he was later hired full-time and now works as a community resource specialist. The KCPL system reaches over 250,000 people, and its Central Library is located in an area with high measures of both poverty and crime. However, over the past decade, Kansas City has seen gentrification in the downtown areas, along with an expansion of new housing options and therefore new communities for the library to serve.

Jason always had a strong desire to work in libraries. While finishing his bachelor's in social work, Jason considered pursuing a master's in library science because he thought it was broad enough to afford him a wide range of professional opportunities within a library system. Then one day he was talking to his social work professor, who knew of a social worker employed by a library. Curious, he did some research and found an article about Mary Olive Joyce, the social worker and director of library outreach and community engagement at KCPL. Looking back on that time, he said, "It just crossed my mind that she was somebody that I wanted to reach out to and get to know, never really thinking there would be an opportunity for an internship. I didn't even know I was going on to get my [MSW] at that point." Mary Olive's role opened Jason's mind to new possibilities, and she was interested in helping shepherd new social workers into library settings.

Jason decided to go on to get his MSW, in part because he had advanced standing from his BSW, allowing him to complete the degree more quickly. At the same time, he applied and was accepted into the AmeriCorps VISTA program, which helped slot him into place at KCPL. Jason was able to complete both his AmeriCorps service and MSW internship at KCPL under Mary Olive's supervision.

Jason said his first social work faculty liaison was very supportive of him doing an internship in the library. She worked with him through the process of developing a learning contract and encouraged him to think of his placement as a legitimate future workplace. Unfortunately, she left half way through the year, and "a few of my other professors couldn't really wrap their

---

1. Jason's story uses real names.

heads around the idea of why I would want to do social work in a library setting. Many view libraries primarily as traditional book depositories rather
than vibrant community hubs which offer programs, services, and resources
for individuals facing life challenges." Over time, Jason was able to show his
faculty the kind of important work he was doing, not only completing his
placement but also leading the way for other students to work in the library:
"They finally got it, and now they're allowing us to host other students. We
have a really good partnership with them."

Initially, developing the learning contract for Jason's time in the library
was very challenging. While it had to reflect the work being done in a library
setting, it also had to demonstrate the social work experiences and skills
required by his MSW program. The library and the school had a lot of conversation about crafting the right language and navigating both library and
social work needs. Mary Olive said that while this was a difficult process, it
"also grew the relationship-building that we had with [the social work fac-
ulty]. . . . Jason's liaison through Park University was very helpful in helping
us navigate that. So I think relationships played a lot in the success." Mary
Olive's unique experience as a trained social worker and long-term library
employee also laid a foundation for Jason's successful internship. "I worked
[in libraries] up until I went and got my master's degree [in social work].
I had worked in four libraries—public, university, and corporate—at different intervals, part-time, throughout my life and love libraries."

As an intern, one of the first things Jason did was conduct a strengths
assessment of each of KCPL's 10 branches. Jason and another AmeriCorps
volunteer spent time interviewing "branch managers and key branch staff to
talk about what they were doing while at their branches, any gaps in services,
what the needs of their patrons were, those kinds of things." After this, Jason
assessed the needs of the branches and developed a prioritized list of the
work he could do during his year as an intern.

One of the top priorities Jason identified was working with individuals
experiencing homelessness. He took a three-pronged approach in response.
First, Jason had heard of other libraries implementing Coffee & Conversation
to build community and provide resources and referrals. Jason learned from a
prior, non-social work intern's struggles to implement it and decided to start by
investing a lot of time "going around and building relationships with individuals who I saw on a daily basis, sort of planting that seed of, 'Hey, I'm going to be
starting this program. Do you think you'd come check it out? This is when it's
going to be.'" When he finally did launch Coffee & Conversation two months
later, he had a dedicated and eager following who attended on a regular basis.
Jason also formed a patron advisory committee with members of the group,
"where we get feedback on what they'd like to see in terms of that programming." Nearly two years later, the program is still in place and running strong.

The second thing Jason did at this internship was assist Mary Olive in bringing service providers to the library who offered "office hours" each week. Jason described it as "a mini-community resource fair on a weekly basis." The providers set up tables in the lobby of the Central Library and met individually with patrons to connect them to resources and services in the community. This has also been a successful program that continues to this day.

The third strategy Jason used to support patrons experiencing homelessness built on a previous internship he had done at a homeless shelter, where he still had positive relationships with youth and staff. He started providing library programming at the shelter during their monthly drop-in event for homeless youth, "so youth that are currently in shelter, youth that were previous clients, and then youth that are currently on the street can drop in and get a free meal and do some sort of activity. We would bring library resources in and do a quick presentation, some sort of game or craft. Now that's been passed on to our youth and family engagement team, who are still doing that."

In addition to meeting the library's assessed needs, it was important to make space for Jason to pursue his interest in gerontology, which was the focus of his MSW studies. As a result, Jason led a meditation group for older adults. He also worked with group home staff members to provide library programming for older adults in a low-income housing complex.

Reflecting on his time as an intern, Jason described success in the diverse experiences he had, as well as his connections with staff and patrons:

> That year of working here really opened my eyes to how lucky I was as a social worker to be able to be in an environment where I have ten different branches I can choose from. I'm working with teens, older adults. You're not discussing one population. So often in social work, you are working in an environment where you focus on a specific population day in and day out. That works for some people, but that would not work for me. I think some of the successes were, in my eyes, just being trusted by staff and library patrons, earning that trust and being a go-to. When somebody needed something they would give me a call. That really indicated to me that I was doing something right, when I started getting those referrals. Also, the fact that I was able to build the relationships that I had with many of our patrons that have lasted to this day was a success to me.

Mary Olive agreed Jason's relationship-building with library staff was important but also thought Jason's work with the community and the community providers was a primary success. She said, "Jason has really built a network of peers [at community organizations] that he relies on, and they rely on him. Through that, we've seen great successes and gains." She feels the welcoming atmosphere Jason helped build has also resulted in a cultural change among library staff: "Coffee & Conversation, really, I felt the change with that . . . and making sure that staff came and staff were invited. There's less references in our incident reports about individuals being crazy and some change in focusing on, 'What can I do in this instance of possible escalation and anger and build on the relationship that I now have with this patron to de-escalate this situation?'"

Despite some great successes, there were also stumbling blocks along the way. Jason described a project he was excited about with the Department of Corrections (DOC) that ended up falling through:

> We were going to work with the Department of Corrections and a local re-entry organization to do videoconferencing to connect parents who are incarcerated with their children here in the city and give them an opportunity to read books together and do weekly visits. In the process of doing that, the DOC had a bunch of turnover in terms of their upper management. . . . So then the project came back around this year, and it looked like we were full steam ahead. Then it has stalled again. [I'm] learning not only within this organization being so large but then working with other large organizations to be patient. Everything doesn't always come out on schedule.

Jason and Mary Olive both agreed consistent supervision and support can be challenging for social work interns in a library setting. Mary Olive explained, "At this department we have so many different things going on. We have four different divisions working on very different focus areas and don't overlap or do overlap. It's easy to get overwhelmed or pulled in different directions and feel like you're on the back burner. . . . Regularly checking in is important to build a solid working relationship and managing the load as well as navigating issues."

Next steps for Jason and Mary Olive include measuring their previous successes, building a trauma-informed library system, and continuing to host MSW interns. In 2017, another intern followed Jason, and in 2018, KCPL plans to host two more social work interns. Jason, who will continue to grow his own experience by supervising interns, said, "We have two interns slated for this fall—one from Park University, one from the University of Kansas. It's going to be a real learning experience for me. It's going to be the first time that I've overseen interns." The interns will be able to focus their projects and work with library staff in their areas of interest.

In contemplating their future work with social work interns, Mary Olive agreed serving the interns' interests as well as the library community's needs benefits everyone involved. She said,

> What I have found most impactful . . . is I want the [intern] to get out of the experience what they're hoping to, and then we will adjust the experience to suit them. They're doing us a huge benefit and helping us build and improve and serve the more vulnerable populations in our community. So I feel like with each person that's coming through, in the long run they

may be asked at some point to vote for the library or speak up for the library or speak up for the individuals that we are serving, and I want to give them a good experience.

Social Work Education: The Basics

As Jason noted when he was trying to figure out which master's degree to pursue, there are a number of similarities between degrees in social work and librarianship, but there are some important differences as well. In this section, we'll look at the structure of social work education and make some comparisons to library programs. While we won't go in depth about curriculum and educational philosophies, it is important to keep in mind our discussion in the introduction on how the alignment of our professional ethics also plays out across the content of our education and the way we think about our roles upon graduation.

Table 3.1 provides an overview of the basic components of each profession's degree programs, including similarities and differences. Some highlights include the fact that a bachelor's degree is available in social work but not librarianship; social work focuses more intensely on the science of human behavior than librarianship does; and, as we're discussing in this chapter, social work students are all required to put in a significant number of internship hours, whereas library students may or may not be required to complete a practicum, depending on their school.

In the same way library schools must be accredited by ALA, schools of social work are accredited by CSWE. As discussed in the preface, state laws vary in who can use the title "social worker," but an accredited degree is a key requirement in all regulations. Accreditation is granted to bachelor's of social work (BSW) and master's of social work (MSW) programs that comply with the accreditation standards established by CSWE. Social work students should ultimately be able to:

1. Demonstrate ethical and professional behavior
2. Engage diversity and difference in practice
3. Advance human rights and social, economic, and environmental justice
4. Engage in practice-informed research and research-informed practice
5. Engage in policy practice
6. Engage with individuals, families, groups, communities, and organizations
7. Assess individuals, families, groups, communities, and organizations
8. Intervene with individuals, families, groups, communities, and organizations
9. Evaluate individuals, families, groups, communities, and organizations (Council on Social Work Education 2015)

Table 3.1   Comparison of Library and Social Work Degree Programs

Profession	Librarianship	Social Work
Degree-accrediting association	American Library Association	Council on Social Work Education
Degree levels recognized in professional accreditation	Master's degrees	Bachelor's and master's degrees
Prerequisites for the master's degree	None	Varies but may include prior coursework in biology, human development, statistics
Typical core courses	History of librarianship or information services, organization of information, research methods, reference services	Interviewing skills, human behavior in the social environment, working with families and groups, working with communities and organizations, research methods, social welfare policy
Practicum or field work requirement	Required only for some programs; not required for accreditation	Considered the "signature pedagogy," extensive hours required at both degree levels, and required for accreditation; explored in detail later in the chapter.

The BSW is considered a "generalist" degree, meaning graduates can apply their social work education within any human service organization at any level of practice: individuals, families, groups, communities, or political systems. At the MSW level, students can continue as advanced generalists or take a more specialized approach, for example, in clinical practice or policy-making. Anyone with a bachelor's degree can apply for an MSW program, but without a BSW, individuals must complete one year of foundational courses on generalist practice social work content. Students with a BSW, like Jason, come in with "advanced standing" and often can skip over the first year, taking less time and fewer credits for MSW completion.

An internship is also a key component of a social work education. An internship involves working in a social service, community, or government agency under the supervision of a professional social worker. The most popular sites for BSW students are child welfare agencies, followed by school social work in K-12 settings, family service agencies, and mental health clinics. At the MSW level, the largest numbers of recent internship placements are in mental health and health settings, followed by schools of social work, and child welfare agencies (Council on Social Work Education 2018).

Interns at the BSW level could begin library work with a focus on making connections between patrons and resources and promoting relationship-building between organizations. MSW students, as "advanced generalists," can also navigate creating community connections and take on a greater degree of interaction with patrons or administrative library work. All social workers are trained to be flexible and operate in environments dealing with constant change and uncertainty.

Collaborating with the School of Social Work

In the United States, there are approximately 500 schools of social work at the undergraduate level and 200 graduate-level programs. If your library is located near an institution that grants bachelor's degrees, there's an excellent chance it has a BSW program or even an MSW program, and online degrees exist as well. As Jakeem said, "We were just so blessed to have a master's of social work program right down the street. We talked about doing an internship program or something like that, but then I thought, well, I would just write a competitive grant proposal for it to see if we could get some actual money, . . . and we did, so that was generative for the program for us." Although his path to collaboration didn't end up involving an intern, his experience shows how easy it can be to connect with a local school of social work and begin collaboration.

The first step to host a bachelor's- or master's-level social work intern is to reach out to a local school and ask for a meeting with the internship coordinator, who may also be known as a field director. Field directors are always on the lookout for new internship sites, which can be a good point of entry for discussion, but librarians should come prepared to give an overview of the benefits the school and their students will get from the library as a host setting. As Jason's experience attests, social work faculty often aren't familiar with this type of placement (though this is rapidly changing), but most will get excited about possibilities once they understand the situation. It's good practice to enter the meeting with the field director prepared to work together on many details of planning the position. Social work internships are great collaborative opportunities but also include many guidelines and requirements laid out by the school and CSWE. Next, we explore the components and considerations to take into account during those conversations.

Internship Purpose and Requirements

CSWE requires students at the BSW level to complete a minimum of 400 hours in an internship, which rises to 900 hours at the MSW level. This means students are at their internship site for a minimum of 12 hours/week and a maximum of 40 hours/week, depending on the timeframe for completion. Internships are usually completed over the course of one or two semesters, during or at the end of the educational program. Internship traditionally involves a concurrent seminar course where students can process their experiences with peers and social work faculty. As part of the seminar course, students relate particular components in their internship to social work concepts. For example, they may need to write about an ethical dilemma that emerges during their practice or reflect upon particular cultural aspects of their work. Many programs will require students to keep logs or journals of their experiences, as well as track the number of hours and activities they perform. Some schools will have students complete specific projects as a part of their internship, such as a social action project, research project, or program evaluation.

The purpose of a social work internship is to give students a real-life experience where they can apply theoretical concepts under supervision before entering professional practice. The ideal social work internship provides students with an opportunity to interact with a variety of people and at different levels of intervention. As explored in chapter 1, social workers are trained to intervene at three levels: micro, mezzo, and macro. Because of the breadth of services the library offers, it can give social work students the opportunity to work within all three arenas. For example, at the micro level, students can work one-on-one with patrons in the library. At the mezzo level, they might help build connections with community partners, like Jason did when he brought his existing relationships with the youth homeless shelter to the library. Students can also help the library "build a case" for having social work services in the library. At the macro level, they can help develop grant proposals, write policy briefs, and design program evaluation.

Many library supervisors go into arranging an internship without knowing the role of a social work field instructor (a different role from field director/internship coordinator), but this is vital information to understand. While a librarian or other library staff member will supervise the social work intern on-site, CSWE requires the student be supervised by a social worker (in some states the social worker must be licensed) in order to receive academic credit for their work. The field instructor is the person who provides that supervision. They work together with the library supervisor and student to develop a learning contract and map out the activities and goals to be accomplished during the internship (a sample learning contract is provided in appendix C and in this chapter's online resources). The field instructor also gives the student important support through reflective supervision (see chapter 6), which helps the student deconstruct and learn from their experiences in order to build emotional resilience. Finally, the field instructor is responsible for making sure the student completes their contract obligations, and they report this information back to the school of social work. The good news is the field instructor's involvement is likely to be more helpful than burdensome to the library supervisor because they handle reporting but don't have to be on-site. Field instructors are used to supervising students at a variety of sites, where day-to-day supervision is delegated to a "task supervisor" who is present in the workplace with the intern and doesn't have to be a social worker. This means the library supervisor as "task supervisor" has control over daily work, and the field instructor can often accomplish their piece of things through meeting for approximately an hour each week with the student.

Regardless of the specific tasks completed by the intern, one unique element to incorporate into any learning contract in a library host setting is education about library culture and librarianship as a profession. Ursula, a library administrator with an MSW, says, "I think that if I would have spent more time at the beginning to learn more about history of libraries and their missions, talking . . . with people from the American Library Association to really digest what it means, it would have made my life much easier, and I would've been more effective." Her reflections are relevant for any social worker who's just entering librarianship. In chapter 4, we'll explore some options for social worker education about librarianship as a critical piece of preparing full-time library social workers, but it's also beneficial to include some form of library professional development opportunity for the intern. This could be as simple as setting aside time for webinars or as integrated as including the student on a presentation to your state's annual library conference. Either way, it's an important piece of the student's learning and can help them bring insights from their social work perspective to your library practice.

Examples of Internship Projects

It's worth noting the amount of work Jason was able to complete during his internship isn't typical. He was working full-time at the library, but many interns will look for something they can do for a couple of days each week. Even with 40 hours a week, Jason struggled to complete everything he wanted to do: "I really thought that I was going to be able to spend more time embedding myself in some of our higher-needs branches. I ended up being really occupied by the programming and the needs here at [the central branch]. . . . When you have nine branches and there's one of you, or 10 branches and there's one of you, . . . [it's difficult] being able to spend more time at the individual branches." Jason provides a great overall example for this chapter because of the variety of tasks he accomplished, but a typical student might tackle one or two of the projects he did. Library managers should be prepared to be flexible about the amount and types of work to be completed, and to discuss those options with the field instructor.

To recap, Jason's projects included:

- Assessment of library community needs at the start of his internship.
- Implementation of Coffee & Conversation by building relationships that would form a foundation of participation before launching the program.
- Coordination of weekly "mini resource fairs" for community organizations in the library.
- Development of his existing relationship with youth experiencing homelessness and their service providers to bring library services to a shelter.
- Leadership and evaluation of meditation programs for older adults in a group home.

As we noted in earlier chapters, there can be overlap between the services provided by students and those offered through social service partnerships. Coffee & Conversation and the office hours or "mini resource fairs" were explored in more detail in chapter 2. Some examples of different areas of focus and service are provided by Amanda, the MSW intern who followed Jason at KCPL. Amanda focused more on services for children and families in the library. Mary Olive, who also supervised Amanda, explained, "What we were seeing is we had individuals who were having their court-appointed supervision in the library. There were things that were happening that were not in accordance with library policy, but then library staff didn't know how to intervene because they knew it was court-appointed. Part of it was there was staff training that needed to take place. Part of it is also a better understanding of what is involved with a court supervision."

Similar to Jason's initial assessment around homelessness, Amanda's first step was asking library staff about their comfort level working with families and parents. She also interviewed families who used the library, talked to other community service providers, and observed staff–patron interactions. One program she developed based on what she learned is the Front Porch Café, which continues to meet weekly. It's facilitated by parents to provide peer support around the challenges of raising kids. Amanda also presented suggestions for policies and programming to the library's administration.

Mary Olive said, "As you know, a public library is a safe place for everybody, whether you're having a good day or a bad day, and our staff will see a bad day situation between a child and their caregiver where it's on the verge of abuse . . . and staff [don't] quite knowing how to intervene or de-escalate." Amanda spent her MSW internship helping to address these issues, and like Jason, was hired full-time to KCPL following her graduation.

Ursula also shared an experience of bringing a social work intern on board to respond to specific community needs: "Two years ago, one of the managers in the old town library was talking a lot about different behaviors that we had from patrons who are experiencing homelessness, . . . and she was saying, 'What can I do? We are seeing behaviors that our librarians are not equipped to deal with. Can you train us?' So we partnered with the university and started an MSW internship. We had an intern that came into the library, and we created very particular outcomes around his intervention for that semester, and we follow that data, and we presented our results. . . . He was very successful, and actually he's working now in the library here." Ursula's example also highlights how a student can be the best option even when a social worker is on staff, as she herself is a social worker, but she didn't have expertise in that particular area.

On a related note, library supervisors and field instructors should work with students to identify and focus on students' strengths in contracted tasks, but they should also be on the lookout for learning opportunities when students are asked to perform unfamiliar tasks. Alecia, a medical social worker who did her MSW practicum in a library, said, "I wish I had more micro level skills, especially responding to people who were in immediate crisis or were having a mental health related crisis in the library. I didn't have experience. You know, I feel like macro and micro tracks [in social work education] are really separated in that way. . . . There were instances where police were called where I didn't really feel like they needed to be called, and I wish that I had had the skills to address those events in different ways." Because students complete these internships toward the end of their degree programs, they may not have the luxury of going back and completing relevant coursework to shore up missing skills. Library supervisors who keep an open and empathetic line of communication can work with the field instructor and student to address these needs as they come up and potentially flag them for follow-up through other partnerships.

With that caveat in mind, social work education provides a broad skill set for students to apply in their internships. As Iris, a social worker who provided library office hours, explained,

No one tells you exactly what you're going to be doing as a social worker when you get that degree because it's a really versatile degree to get. So I think my professors did a pretty good job of just teaching me flexibility and going with the flow. One thing that happened when we first started the collaborative was I was just kind of dumbfounded that people were going to let me do this. I mean, yeah, I never thought I could take that much initiative and just start something, but if you see a need, go ahead and just start something and take care of the issue.

Iris also pointed out students may need some prompting to find the confidence to improvise with their skills in a library, just as they would when adapting to any host setting: "I don't think it's necessarily communicated to our undergrads. I think they would think, 'Oh well, someone has to direct me,' or, 'You know, my program will have laid out what I'm going to do,' but actually in my current job, and in a lot of my colleagues' jobs, you see a need, and you mold your profession around that, and things are constantly changing." When that support for student confidence is in place, interns can accomplish great things. Vivian, a librarian said, "We got a second year master's student last year, and she was great. She basically built this program from the ground up, like we had help from her supervisor at the Department of Health and Human Services, but we didn't really have anything to go on because nobody in the state has done this before. She's done a great job pulling it together, and basically her job is to connect people to area resources but to do so with a human touch so nobody has to make that first phone call by themselves."

To conclude, one thing Jason learned is genuine, relationship-based change takes time. Jason said, "I told [Amanda] that when you're building capacity and it's slow-moving, it's not like that checklist that we've talked about. . . . You don't have that satisfaction at the end of the day. But knowing what you're building is going to be lasting and solid, . . . hopefully you're around to see it come to fruition." This is also important for library supervisors to remember when they're designing and guiding a student contract, and it's helpful to pause from time to time and remember this is a long-term process.

Academic Librarians and Social Work Students

Academic librarians who work as liaisons to schools of social work have a special role to play in fostering library-social work collaboration. We encourage social work liaison librarians to engage in a couple of different ways to reach both professors and students and help bridge social work education into library practice.

One area of need we touched on at the start of this chapter is simply building awareness among social work faculty. Ryanne, an academic librarian who is a social work liaison, explained to us this is something she has been working on as well: "I'm still interested in bringing awareness to my institution in terms of the field placement office and raising awareness for them that placing social work student in libraries, in public libraries in particular, or school libraries, is a real, valid option in terms of students who are on a community organizing track or in a community mental health track. But especially as we're seeing a growing interest in that collaboration between public libraries and social work, [we need] to utilize those students better." Tyra, who completed her MSW internship in a library, backed this up: "My field director had no idea really what was going on at the library. It was very new to her. So, if there was a way to let social work programs know more that this is something happening . . . I mean it's new, but it's not extremely new. So network that out, and let them know what the program is about and how it can benefit students." Not only are social work librarians well positioned to share information on library field placements because of their connections with many faculty and students, but they can also help evaluate impact and design responsive curricula based on expanding into library host settings.

Social work librarians face human service needs as well as information needs from students. The majority of social work students come to the field wanting to "help people." They tend to be caring, empathetic, and passionate individuals. But they don't always have a clear idea what that really means or how they will be a part of that process. Many social work students are surprised to learn they're required to take courses in research, policy, economics, and biology. Students can easily feel daunted by the rigors of creating research proposals, identifying social problems, and developing policy interventions. While social work instructors can help with this process, they are often more focused on the content and less on the process of finding the needed information and sifting through resources to determine their accuracy and validity. Simply providing the information literacy and research services academic librarians may consider routine can make the difference between success or failure for social work students. As a social work professor, Mary has been astonished to learn all the ways her liaison librarian can support her and her students. Her librarian helped design and edit assignment rubrics and research guides, recommended films, ordered journals, lectured in classes, and met with students to further develop their research topics. An interactive research guide from one of Mary's classes can be found in the online resources. Building these relationships can also lay the foundation for faculty to better understand libraries as potential host sites.

At the same time as students start to engage with clients and their rich, challenging life experiences, they can quickly face emotional burnout. Ryanne pondered, "How well are we equipped to serve [social work] students, and how are their needs potentially different or unique than what might come up in the context of a reference consultation . . . with a law student, or business student, or a student of a different discipline?" Social work librarians ask these kinds of questions because they see the need for whole person support of their student patrons. Quincy, another social work librarian, said, "I feel like we spend a lot of time with helping students or pushing back with students, going, 'This is what I can help you with. This is what you need to go talk to your advisor about, or you need to go talk to the faculty about,' and just helping them maybe even frame what they need to talk to them about." Much like the information literacy instruction noted earlier, this can be an experience of academic librarians that stretches beyond social work students, but the intensity of social work's human connections can make it feel especially pressing. Ryanne also noted, "Even way more so now than when I was in [social work] school 15–16 years ago, is the pressures on the student, the economic pressures, the compassion fatigue, the stuff that they're facing in their placements. I think that is just a cocktail sometimes of burnout early on before they even graduate." Social work librarians see this side of students where faculty may not, and it presents an opportunity for developing their own research into providing library-based supports and referrals for social work students.

Online Resources

www.wholepersonlibrarianship.com/book/resources/chapter3

- Links to
    - CSWE and ALA accreditation guidelines
    - Social work students and public libraries
    - Librarian-created course guide for one of Mary's social work classes
- Learning contract template for a social work student in a public library (also see appendix C)
- Additional resources provided by you and your colleagues

CHAPTER FOUR

Full-Time Library Social Workers

I think the challenge that probably most folks would say, including Chloe, is that we only have one Chloe.

—Kai, public librarian

Overview

This chapter brings us to the ultimate partnership: a full-time social worker in the library. There are many important details to explore here, from the logistics of funding, to the culture of staff integration, to the social worker's tasks and professional development needs. Hiring and integrating an entirely new type of library staff member takes a lot of work but can produce equally significant results for your community and staff.

We start with the story of a library social worker who had good support from both the library and her nonprofit employer but still did a lot of learning on the fly as she built a successful outreach model. Next, we review what has become the classic model of a full-time library social worker at SFPL and explore how other systems, including the one in this chapter's major example, have adopted or modified this model to fit their own needs. Through that exploration, we'll break down some of the key elements to consider in designing your own position. From there, we move on to hiring logistics and data collection, then finish with some tips for making your library hospitable to its new social worker.

Ashley's Story

Ashley Horn[1] serves as the only full-time library social worker at Brooklyn Public Library (BPL). Ashley moved to New York City after working as a clinical social worker in other large cities, serving people struggling with addiction, homelessness, and mental health concerns. When she was looking for a new job, she was intrigued by the opportunity at BPL. She said,

> The library was always my place. This job kind of ruined the library for me personally [*laughing*], just because I know everyone in every branch, so I can't really hang out without seeing people I work with, but I love the library. I always spent all my time there, just using it as a patron, going to composting classes and just whatever. [When I lived in other places], I was a member of the library, I checked out books and used the library. And when I saw this position, I thought it looked really interesting, and it was different.

Ashley's position is part of a contract between the library and Breaking Ground, a large nonprofit that provides services to individuals experiencing chronic and long-term homelessness. The library system pays for Ashley's salary, and Casey, her supervisor at Breaking Ground, oversees the program. According to Casey, Breaking Ground started to notice that a growing number of its clients experiencing homelessness were spending all day in the library because it was a "safe space, it was quiet, and they were able to—they just feel safe there and feel like they could be there and not be bothered, but [they] also could access information and could maybe get some help in a more low-key sort of way." Breaking Ground worked with the different library branches informally to provide services to patrons, gradually coming to understand that a more formal and permanent relationship would better serve the individuals being seen by both organizations. Casey reflected, "It just became apparent that it would be a really good resource for us to be officially and directly connected within the library system to try and reach as many people as possible. We had a big expansion of our program back in 2016, which is also when this program started. And our goal, as always, is to just be able to get into every institution where homeless people might be living, and so we work a lot with hospitals and libraries and different governmental facilities, trying to make sure we're not missing anyone."

At the same time as Breaking Ground was expanding, one of the BPL managers was researching and planning to build a program similar to the one at SFPL, described in the next section of this chapter. A survey of library

---

1 Ashley's story uses real names.

staff showed strong interest in starting an outreach services department. Eighty-five staff members attended the first outreach services department meeting, which focused on homeless services and addressing homelessness in the public library. Breaking Ground came to that meeting to talk about its program, and this served as the first step in a more formal arrangement between the library and the nonprofit. Ongoing conversations and planning continued, which ultimately led to Ashley's hire as the library social worker in 2016.

According to Ashley, "It was a good fit for me in terms of needing to be a proactive kind of person who is starting a program that doesn't exist, so we're all just coming up with ideas, and it felt really 'piloty' and 'grass-rootsy,' kind of flexible and creative." She made a point of visiting all 60 branches in her first few months on the job. She reflected, "I just went out to every single branch, made sure the staff knew I was there and how they could reach me, [and I would] talk to them about any patrons that were struggling. I [also] felt comfortable approaching patrons right away."

Despite Ashley's enthusiasm, some challenges did emerge. Ashley said in the beginning, patrons were often ambivalent or confused by her role at the library, and she also had to navigate relationships with clients who already knew Breaking Ground from other situations. Ashley spent a great deal of her time talking to library directors and staff about her role and about "the values of librarianship and the understanding of privacy and the comfort level and expectation of privacy in the library. I mean, initially when I would walk into a branch, I would be like, 'Hi, I'm Ashley, and I want you to know we have social work support in the library. Do you need anything?' I would connect with the patrons in a way that the library staff don't necessarily engage." Eva, BPL's outreach services director, said this was something they also worked on with library staff: "One thing we talk about sometimes is even the difference of the question of 'Can I help you?' or 'What are you looking for?' versus [the fact that] libraries aren't usually in the habit of asking, 'Are you okay?'" Ashley agreed that library staff are "not necessarily going to try to engage in a social work way, interviewing [patrons] or asking if they need help with anything and connecting them with a resource."

Another challenge was creating and reconciling the data collection practices of BPL and Breaking Ground. The library was not equipped to track its patrons on whether they were receiving social services. "We wouldn't track or even want to have access to [patron data]," Eva said. Yet, to provide services and demonstrate the success of the program, it has been necessary to communicate and record relevant data, such as whether a person is homeless and has been connected to case management. This is because in order to qualify for transitional housing in New York City, an individual must be verified as being chronically street homeless.

Breaking Ground has a contract with the City of New York to provide homeless outreach services and access to a large city database, which contains information on all the shelter programs, individuals making use of services, and people experiencing street homelessness in the five-borough area around Brooklyn. Getting these reports allowed Breaking Ground to more quickly connect library patrons with housing. Ashley said this approach has worked better in the library than on the streets: "We've known them on the street, maybe, but we've connected with them more in the library system and been able to place them into our transitional housing programs and start working through the process and getting them ID and benefits and medical assistance and everything else that they need, and then working towards their permanent housing goals, whatever those might be."

Librarians were also able to track the contacts they made and the referrals they gave to patrons. Eva explained,

[In] our system, we do track referrals, for instance, that are being made. In our regular database system, it's not a super specific referral list; it's just like we took the person to get a birth certificate, vital records, appointments, stuff like that. It's pretty general. But we've found that the people the library staff were seeing were asking for different services and asking for a lot more specific services. So we had to spend some time figuring out a better way to track our referrals. We only recently started that. So I feel like it's a work in progress, definitely. We're working on a monthly report that we are able to send to the library side of things and the Breaking Ground side of things so that our higher-ups can know the work we're doing, get a picture of the successes and the actions we're able to take, let us know what adjustments we need to make, and [ask] if they have questions.

Casey corroborated the collaborative value of data collection: "As you probably know, you could have like a million spreadsheets just rumbling around in the universe and not really doing the job that we're trying to get better, like where we're collecting things and making sure that everybody is doing things the same way. . . . We have a data person on our end at Breaking Ground. She's working with me and Ashley to make sure that everything is user-friendly and contains continuity across the board."

While connecting with patrons experiencing homelessness has been the primary goal of Ashley's position, she has also provided important training and support to frontline library staff. Breaking Ground and BPL Outreach Services designed and offered training opportunities for staff to help them feel more engaged and empowered to interact with patrons. Casey explained, "What we've seen in the life of this program has been the need to be flexible and creative and thoughtful about our approach and about what we're offering and just [be] open to whatever comes our way. I feel like that's the homeless outreach philosophy, but it's been especially concentrated in the library."

Ashley said this kind of training has been incredibly successful in helping to change hearts and minds when it comes to interacting with patrons experiencing homelessness or other challenges:

> I've seen a shift in just the time I've been at the library in people's openness to engaging someone experiencing homelessness, like maybe a reduction in their fear around mental health and more appropriately handling situations, or even like reaching out to Breaking Ground and having some better expectations and understanding of what the options are. . . . [I model] the one-on-one interactions that I sometimes bring the staff into and introduce regular patrons to the staff, so they've been able to build a relationship with someone who's in the branch every day who they might have not talked to before.

Eva said reducing stigma was one of the primary goals of the partnership, and she has definitely seen movement in this area, especially staff being willing to engage more proactively with patrons: "There's not as much helplessness or sense of issues being too complicated. People are more informed and aware of the different dynamics, even around hygiene and smell, which is often something that people feel really uncomfortable talking about or aren't sure what the action is that they need [to take]."

Ashley believes having a social worker in the library has been a catalyst for staff to communicate more of the issues they face in the library: "I do think it's opened up the floodgates of all these things that are occurring in the system for the higher administration to understand the need that staff is reporting. I think definitely the staff used me at the beginning as a way to communicate what they needed to support patrons and what the struggles were they were having in the branches. So I think that has allowed for further programs and further resources and other kinds of options for training." One example she offered was a training on administering Narcan that was open to both staff and the public at the Library. Over 100 people attended. While she considered that training a success, Ashley said there are still tensions for some staff who feel providing this kind of intervention goes beyond what should be required of them within their job. Ashley said the level of need is large, but the number of staff ready to meet the need is small: "Some of the staff still really want our team to come out, or they want Breaking Ground to come out every single time they call. I don't know if it's a comfort level or if there's a boundary with their role, but there is still some discomfort and resistance, I would say, to using the resources that are available [to them on their own] and taking action and doing whatever you need to do, whether to be trained or help someone."

The level of emotional support needed by library staff is another aspect of the library-social work partnership that has needed to be addressed. Eva said,

> One thing we've been talking about is . . . the best use of a social worker's time versus what are things that we should build capacity in other areas of the organization, or what are things that require training of our public safety staff. So it's also figuring out how to make sure that Ashley doesn't become sort of a crisis worker. People really value her perspective when dealing with all kinds of really challenging things. Mental illness comes to mind as one of the biggest ones. Staff will often reach out to her just to get her perspective on something. I think we're trying to figure out how to sort of set parameters around that, or also how to figure out how to build other supports for staff, even around staff wellness and the stress of providing services to people who have really acute needs, like Ashley pointed out, how much social work has built into the profession certain kinds of peer support and self-care that is expected. Those things have not developed in the same way in the library profession, even as libraries have shifted to become these community spaces where librarians are addressing every day people with all kinds of different social support needs.

Ashley acknowledged how challenging this has been for her, as well as the need for her to enforce boundaries around her role in the library: "I used to do a drop-in for staff where people would come and express all of their issues, like someone came and asked for a book about suicide, and I don't think I did the right thing. I think they were crying out for help, but I don't know. I just showed them the book. I feel bad about it now. [Library staff] would drop in and talk to me about anything. I thought it was a good plan at the beginning. . . . Then I realized that other library social workers weren't doing that because they saw those people as their colleagues."

One of the exciting things to come from this challenge is recognition of the types of support that library staff need when they're providing public services. Eva explained,

> Sometimes [the need for support] comes up as the desire to have more coverage of public safety officers. That's something that staff will ask for. But one of the things that I think is real exciting that has shifted is that the institution as a whole and people who make decisions about hiring and strategies are talking more about, "What if we didn't have more public safety officers—what if we had ten more social workers?" A lot of the issues that we're seeing [are] issues around an acute need or behavior that a lot of times is actually support that's needed and a shared strategy among staff, rather than having more [law] enforcement.

There are a number of ways the logistics of the BPL-Breaking Ground partnership set up Ashley for ongoing success. Ashley pointed out that having a social work supervisor, rather than someone from a library-only background, has been a key support. Casey from Breaking Ground has been Ashley's supervisor even though she doesn't work directly in the library, and she would meet with Ashley every week to discuss ongoing programming, challenges, and next steps. Ashley said, "It's really unique—I'm the only social worker in the system, so you need to have connection to other social workers, which is something that I definitely miss in this role sometimes, other people doing this kind of work. That for me comes through the other library social workers and partners." Ashley also meets at least once a week with the other street outreach workers connected to library patrons experiencing homelessness.

Ashley also talked about the importance of having the support of the library system and library administrators who are willing to hear and act upon feedback from staff and patrons. She said,

> I think the library system has to be on board and want someone to come into the library and do this. So I've definitely talked with other library social workers who don't necessarily have that support from their system. I think that can be really tricky. I, for the most part, receive really great feedback from staff that they're so happy working there. They're so grateful for the kind of work we're doing. They're appreciative of when you come out or when you do a training. I think the staff wish there were more support, more social workers, but our team does too.

When asked what the future holds for the partnership, Ashley laughingly said, "Thirty social workers!" In support of a continued and possibly expanded library-social work collaboration at BPL, Ashley and other staff continuously document outcomes that demonstrate the need as well as the benefit of having a social work on staff. Eva said the library is trying to get "a picture of what is happening and then see if there are certain things that stick out as the most immediate and that make the most sense in terms of investing more, or which things could be better distributed through Breaking Ground or through other library programs." Ashley agreed and said, "I just think that having a social worker in the library system is a benefit. I think there's a lot of good things that can come from it. So I think that it's great that so many libraries are thinking about having a social worker or some kind of outreach. I think you're meeting patrons where they already are, so I think it's just a really obvious place to put someone."

The Classic Model: San Francisco Public Library

Ashley talked about using the model provided by SFPL in designing her position, explaining that the librarian who initially championed her position "had a whole file when I started that he went over with me, and he had done extensive research. Basically, he saw one of Leah's PBS shows or something that she did an interview for. He was fascinated with the idea. And he had done a ton of research on what other library social workers were doing and what the programs look like and how he would model like this." By the time this book is published, Leah Esguerra will have been SFPL's full-time, on-site social worker for a decade. When she was hired in 2009, she and SFPL created her role from scratch, and it has since served as a template and inspiration for many other libraries besides BPL.

Leah's responsibilities cover each of the micro, mezzo, and macro areas of responsibility in social work:

1. Micro: Supervise Health and Safety Associates (HASAs). These part-time outreach workers circulate through the Central Library during all open hours. They interact with patrons and offer resources around shelter and basic needs, if those concerns arise. They all have a personal connection to experiencing homelessness. Typically, there are four of them employed at any given time. Leah also is on call to assist with crisis management and case referrals for patrons in the library.

2. Mezzo: Educate and support library staff members. This includes more formal education and discussion around issues like TIC (see chapter 1), mental health, and substance abuse, as well as informal consultations to help staff process challenging patron encounters and strategize for future interactions. This work happens in conjunction with strategic directions for the library system as a whole.

3. Macro: Advocate for the library and advise on strategic change. Leah has the same level of access to government resources as any other social work manager in the city. She sits on government committees and meets and coordinates with partnering organizations. She also works with library management on strategic decisions in library policy and practice.

These micro, mezzo, and macro tasks play out in nearly every full-time social work position, though they can take different forms. Your library system will need to consider priorities to determine how much emphasis to place on the tasks that are most important to you, as well as how to structure and invest staff time.

Micro: Outreach and Crisis Management

Outreach by social workers and related staff in libraries happens primarily at the micro level, through one-to-one interactions. This creates a human connection between staff members and patrons. It helps patrons feel safer to bring their unique needs and circumstances into the library. Information sharing in a relationship-based reference collection, as described in chapter 1, is an extension of this outreach, where workers provide materials about local resources, facilitate a "warm hand-off" to someone at another organization, or escalate the patron to the library social worker for more complex case management and referral. Social workers also have their version of applying a library model, as described by Yusef, a library social worker:

> We kind of see ourselves like librarians, in the idea that if someone comes up and asked you for a book, you give them what they need, and you may point out some other things that might help out. So that is the model of social work we like in the library, following the library model. So if someone comes in, and they want boots, we are going to get them boots. And hopefully the relationship will improve, and maybe they will want clothing as well, and that will build from there, but we always go with what the patron wants.

In San Francisco, frontline outreach is performed by staff members who aren't credentialed social workers but do have a personal connection to the community they serve. This is similar in some respects to library-social work partnerships with nonprofits, where outreach workers come to the library to connect patrons to resources but then return to their home organizations, as explored in chapter 2. Hosting outreach workers in-house means they can be present regularly and predictably, helping to meet SFPL's extensive patron needs and provide visibly reliable access to care. Delegating routine introductions and information-sharing to the HASAs has the benefit of patron first contact being with someone "like them," while also freeing Leah's time for her community and strategic responsibilities. Leah participates in this micro-level work by being available on call to help with crisis management and de-escalation as needed.

The lead social worker at another major urban library system that modeled its structure on SFPL, Zelda, describes her outreach setup:

> We have [two] social workers, and we also have five peer navigators and are modeling after San Francisco. So, the peer navigators are people who are living in recovery with life experiences of homelessness, living with a mental health diagnosis, maybe a substance use issue, justice involvement, things like that, and have gone to a training through a peer run agency here . . . to work with other people and connect on that peer-to-peer level to engage them and help support them in achieving whatever their goals might be and building those relationships with the customers. . . . What we do is provide outreach throughout mostly our central location, our building downtown, and then a fewer branches that are closer to downtown . . . asking [people] how they're doing, asking them if they need

anything, provide them with some socks or a water bottle, and then the peer navigators have the social worker's card. . . . So people learn about us, not only from our outreach and advertising our drop-in hours on some calendars around the building, but also if someone has a question that they ask the library staff, or the library staff or security recognizes something that we can help with, they refer the people to us. So either they send them to us, or they call, and we go down and meet the person where they are.

Libraries in large urban areas often emulate this model, or they may employ social work interns who are supervised by the library's full-time social worker to accomplish outreach tasks in lieu of or in addition to peer navigators. In smaller systems or locations with different levels of need, the social worker's role might encompass or even prioritize this micro-level work. On the flip side, some systems choose to employ a full-time social worker whose primary responsibilities are at a macro level and involve strategizing how to support systematic change in library education and culture to better support patrons with diverse needs. That person may spend very little time in the micro role. How this plays out in your library will depend on the needs you identify for your community, the budget you secure, and the availability of potential project partners.

One thing to consider when staffing for micro-level work is long-term sustainability. Some libraries have hired outreach workers similar to the HASAs or peer navigators but without the oversight of a full-time social worker. This can be a tempting option for libraries with limited budgets, but the results can be unpredictable, and staff turnover in such roles tends to be high. Elana, director of a large, urban library system, shared her frustrations with taking on a staff member in that type of role: "We've had mixed experiences with the partnership we have in terms of the skills and ability of the navigators. . . . The first navigator we had was outstanding—so outstanding she ended up getting a job with another agency. The second and third and maybe fourth navigators, we had trouble: they didn't show up, they were not very well trained, it was all of that. Now we have somebody who is really outstanding, and of course we spend a lot of time worrying that he is going to disappear." Similarly, Kai described how her system saw the need to upgrade the expertise of their social worker following her initial hire: "[The outreach worker] has a bachelor's in social work, but she has a lot of background in doing this work, and she's doing a really great job. However, we did this year put in a request to the city for more funding . . . and so the funding level that we have now would be for someone that does have an MSW."

Still, there are plenty of library social workers who provide micro service as part or even the majority of their work. Leslie, whose advocacy work we explore in chapter 5, is one such example. Anya, a social worker in a first-ring suburb, is another: "I do outreach to homeless individuals or people who come into the library who look like they need help. I just walk around and ask how they are doing, let them know I am a social worker if they need referrals." She recognized the immense value of this level of service to both staff and patrons in her comments as well, saying that "librarians have said that it's just nice to have somebody that they can call when . . . they don't know what to do with someone or they don't know how to best help that person. If there is a question about benefits, or someone is interested in looking for guardianship, or somebody needs to supply for food stamps or Medicaid, I am someone that they can call to help them right on the spot." This is the exact work many library social workers are initially hired to accomplish.

Mezzo: Community Connections and Case Referrals

Mezzo-level work builds a bridge from micro to macro. For library social workers, this includes engaging in staff education. They design, coordinate, and offer training sessions, and they coach and sometimes challenge the assumptions of administrators and managers. They give staff the tools they need for interacting with patrons, coping with the aftermath of challenging situations, and preventing burnout. Ultimately, all of this serves patrons as well as staff members by fostering an inclusive, compassionate space.

Library social workers are often hired in response to patron needs, but they come to see very quickly that staff need support as well. Chue described that at his library: "I think there's some knowledge [of how to work with challenging patrons], but there's also just kind of fear. Burned out people want somebody else to handle some of these issues. These are complicated issues that without training and without knowledge, you are not going to be able to deal with." In her library system, Anya offers a variety of support: "I have done staff trainings around how to set boundaries with patrons, how to work with patrons who are dealing with a mental health crisis. I am doing a training next week on how to work with patrons on the autism spectrum that I think people have found really helpful." Library social workers can also delegate some of this work and help keep their workload manageable by using their professional contacts to find experts to lead sessions on specific topics. Bradley, a social worker in a suburban library system, described his use of outside training to bring TIC to his staff: "We started out with trauma-informed care in our department and an offer to all staff of overall mental health first aid, and we are about to be trained in QPR, so question persuade and refer, and it is a type of training that actually trains non-clinicians to have baseline engagement skills with people experiencing mental illness."

As Ashley discovered, though, coaching and mentoring staff can be a slippery slope to becoming a staff therapist, which burns out the social worker and keeps them from attending to patron needs. That's something for all new library social workers and their library manager counterparts to keep in mind, and we talk about it more in a later section on setting boundaries. The social worker is the guide, but ultimately, cultural change requires that all staff members take charge of their own experiences. Bradley explained that before he started his role, "For years, patrons experiencing poverty or homelessness with co-occurring issues of mental health issues attached to substance abuse would utilize [the library], so they needed various continuums of care that really the traditional library format or system could not provide." Mezzo-level work is very much about placing the library within a continuum of care, which happens through relationship-building with other organizations.

This type of relationship-building is similar to the role we discussed for library staff in chapter 1, but it goes above and beyond transactional referral to a deeper connection within the social service community. As we will discuss further in the following sections on data collection and choosing an employment home, social workers have access to personal information about patrons and clients that library staff members can't and shouldn't see. Cyndi shared an example: "Just this morning, I had a young woman here who really needed some outreach, so I called . . . a local agency that works with youth experiencing homeless, and they were really great. The fact that not only do we have internal support from our staff, but then outside support, is huge."

Library social workers foster these organizational connections in addition to sustaining one-to-one relationships with peers at complementary organizations. The knowledge base that library social workers build through these interactions enables them to make their own accurate referrals at the micro level as well as train other employees on available resources. In turn, community partners learn to see the library as part of the same continuum of care. As Yusef explained, "Other agencies have been really receptive to helping the library. People love the library, and they reduce barriers for us, things we normally wouldn't be able to do in our day-to-day work on the streets." When library social workers build relationships with other social workers, they're part of a mezzo-level network of access to case management systems, which is important to how they understand and navigate the landscape of social services.

Macro: Systematic Change

Macro-level work happens at a cultural or societal level. To the extent that library social workers create a cultural shift through training library staff, that role could be considered to have a macro as well as mezzo impact. Leah is increasingly involved at a macro level through coaching library systems that want to hire social workers and mentoring new library social workers. Similarly, library social workers' connections with other organizations can also lead to macro-level impact, particularly when they're positioned at a higher administrative level. By virtue of being in a management position, Zelda explained, she's "able to be in a lot of meetings and really help to make decisions in regards to what the library will be doing with certain things and keep a trauma-informed social work focus on some of those things and how we are best serving our customers."

Like Zelda, many library social workers play an important role in library culture by helping to (re)develop equitable library policies. Using her perspective as a social worker and psychologist, Ursula has worked with her library board, which "is very supportive of us, and we are trying to pass a policy that is talking specifically about evaluating our services, collections, and programs. . . . The other piece was really about providing multicultural and equitable services and programs, what that looks like, and what kind of training do we need. When we say we are welcoming to all, what does that look like when it comes to our families and the way we talk to patrons and the way we create our programs?" Her library administration hadn't considered getting involved with policymaking outside the library system until she came on board. Her role "put us in a platform we weren't in before. We are now able to have conversations with city council members, with the United Way, more macro-level in the community. They're bringing us the conversation that they didn't used to before in terms of budgeting or how the school district is thinking about programs for bilingual household reading acquisitions. That didn't happen before. I don't think the library saw themselves as having a role at those levels, at those tables."

Just as Zelda's efforts opened up a new role for her library's administrators as community change agents, all social workers have much to teach librarians about macro-level work. Chapter 5 goes into greater depth on the kind of policymaking and advocacy social workers provide, what that looks like in a library setting, and how it might be adapted for greater reach in librarianship.

Logistics of the Hire

Like every other aspect of this work, there's no single approach for justifying and financing a library social worker. In many cases, the solution libraries are able to piece together comes back to the relationships they have with community and government partners. Ashley's position, funded by the library but run through Breaking Ground, is a fairly typical example. It's also important to remember that even current full-time library social workers may not yet have a permanent funding source. Per a 2018 scan of 36 news items announcing the formation of library-social work collaborations, the average age of programs at that time was two years, which is also the length of many initial contracts for hire. Yusef, who helped found an outreach center in a library, described designing these programs as "building the plane while we're flying it." We're still waiting to see how many of those planes will be able to land and take off again.

Throughout the preceding chapters, we've emphasized relationship-building and documenting the impact of your partnerships. If your library system wants to hire a full-time social worker, this is where that work can pay off. It's increasingly common for libraries to host interns or office hours like those explored in the preceding chapters in order to craft a solid base of documented need. Vivian is one of many librarians who took this first step: "We did part of this project to determine, 'Oh, do we need a social worker?' and we determined within the first six weeks, not only do we need a social worker, we need two full-time social workers." By keeping track of the number and type of interactions her student interns had, along with the number of referrals they made, Vivian was able to justify and secure a two-year grant to contract a full-time social worker in her library. Leslie, whose story is featured in the next chapter, is an example of a similar success through first documenting the impact of social service office hours.

It's not always necessary to start with an intern or office hours. Now that more libraries of all sizes are hiring social workers, administrators can look to successful peer programs to provide justification for creating their own. However, libraries often choose the further intermediate step of hiring their first full-time social worker on a contract for one or two years. This has been the case for new social workers in St. Paul, Los Angeles, Anchorage, and Tulsa, just to name a few. In fact, immediately permanent positions, like those in San Francisco or Washington, D.C., tend to be the exception, not the rule. The benefit of a contract or temporary pilot position is that it gives the project more flexibility, and the employee can start more quickly than a traditional hire. The library, funder, and partners can take time during the contract period to thoroughly assess and document community need and best practices before committing to a permanent program. The downside is the possibility that funding may not be available for the position to continue in the long run. As Zelda explained, her system is "definitely trying to figure out how these positions [that I supervise] will continue to be funded. . . . We hope to sustain that funding, but if we don't, then we lose those positions as well . . . and so I think that's something for libraries to really consider as well as how to sustain that, because once you start it, it's going to be really hard to take that away." Libraries and partners who implement a pilot program should consider the potential negative community impact and begin planning for sustainability as soon as the new social worker is hired.

It's also important to frame how you think of your new hire so they align with the demographics of the community needing help. Lily, branch manager of a library with a social worker on staff, recommended you "know your demographic and keep in mind cultural sensitivity. It's unfortunate, but certain professional phenotypes will be a barrier, like where I am people have been deported, and so there's distrust for a 56-year-old male of European descent. The person we hired is Latina, she's fluent [in Spanish], and she's a female. . . . People just go by faith in knowing the climate of your demographic." As we mentioned at the start of the book, social workers, like librarians, don't entirely reflect the demographics of the people they serve, so it's not always possible to make a perfect match. Depending on the flexibility of your hiring scheme, you might also face some limitations on how much weight you can give to someone's personal background, as compared to other job qualifications. All of which is to say: if you end up hiring someone from outside your primary community, it can be successful, but you'll want to work with that person to plan integration of the community into your services. One example of this is Leah's supervision of the HASAs at SFPL: they share a background of experiencing homelessness with the patrons they serve. You can also specifically seek out social work students in your community to work as interns under the library social worker's supervision. This doubles your impact by reflecting the community in your staff while also supporting diversity in social work as a profession.

Host Organizations and Funding

Whether social workers are hired temporarily or permanently, their funding streams can originate in and flow through any number of entities. Long-term relationships with community partners may yield opportunities to hire their staff members in the library. Some of the other options listed here, such as government agencies or libraries themselves, can be the funding source as well as the employment home for the social worker. However, especially when the initial appointment is on contract, it's just as likely that two or three partners can be involved. Zelda gives one example: "Our student social work positions are library employees, but our peer navigators are grant funded, and they're actually employed by another agency and contracted to work with us here." In Table 4.1, we explore some pros and cons of the various types of host organizations. For the purpose of this discussion, we're defining host organization as the entity officially employing the social worker, which may be different from the funding source or actual work location.

There are a few main issues we've taken into consideration with these pros and cons:

- **Access to Case Management Systems:** Social workers need access to case management systems in order to do their most effective work, but because of the highly confidential nature of case file content, agencies are careful about issuing permissions. Slotting the social worker into an existing position type or classification that comes with case file access—often an option through nonprofits or government agencies—can be an easy way to make sure that access is covered. If the social worker is in a contract position or role that doesn't have access, hiring managers should work with partners on how to secure it.

Table 4.1   Comparison of Host Organizations

Host Organization: Library

Pros	Cons
• Keeps supervision in-house. • Library managers can make decisions without as much partner consultation. • Social worker benefits from integration into library staff culture, following the same rules and norms. • If the initial hire is temporary, may set the groundwork for sustainability.	• Library managers may not understand how a social worker functions professionally and therefore may not be able to offer fulsome workplace support. • Social worker may not have access to case management systems unless special arrangements are made. • Bureaucratic hurdles may slow down hiring and changes, depending on funding stream.

Host Organization: Municipal Government

Pros	Cons
• Many social workers are already employed by city or county government agencies, giving library social worker a professional peer group. • Typically means social worker has access to the same case management systems as peers. • Provides an opportunity for other government agencies to learn about the library and be directly involved in benefits of connecting with clients in that setting.	• Library managers may not have direct supervision of the social worker and therefore may have less control over their work. • Requires additional library effort to communicate outcomes to the host agency in order to secure continued support. • Bureaucratic hurdles may slow down hiring and changes, depending on funding stream.

Host Organization: Nonprofit Agency

Pros	Cons
• Similar to employment through municipal government, it provides a social work peer group and case management system access.	• Library managers may not have direct supervision of social worker and may have less control over their work.

Host Organization: Nonprofit Agency

Pros	Cons
• May offer more flexible hiring terms than a government agency (including the library), which can be useful for jump-starting an initial contract. • Can potentially build on existing partnerships and expand future partnerships, further embedding the library in continuum of care.	• Requires additional library effort to communicate outcomes to the host agency in order to secure continued support. • Staff turnover at nonprofits can be high, which means priorities (as well as supervision) can change quickly. • Funding may be insecure, depending on funding stream.

Hiring Organization: State or Regional Library System

Pros	Cons
• Creates opportunity for several libraries or library systems to share social work services. • May foster greater collaboration between state agencies. • Social worker benefits from integration into library staff culture, following the same rules and norms. • If the initial hire is temporary, it may set the groundwork for sustainability.	• Library managers may not understand how a social worker functions professionally and therefore may not be able to offer fulsome workplace support. • Library branch managers may not have direct supervision of social worker and may have less control over their work. • Social worker may not have access to case management systems unless special arrangements are made. • Bureaucratic hurdles may slow down hiring and changes, depending on funding stream.

- **Library Culture and Social Work Professional Peer Groups:** We explore this in-depth in a later section on supporting the social worker. Hiring managers need to be mindful of the fact that library social workers can feel very isolated if they don't have access to social work peers. Library managers should also be proactive about how to introduce the social worker to library culture, educate library staff on the social worker's role, and prepare library supervisors to support social workers (if needed).

- **Flexibility and Sustainability of Hire:** Library and government bureaucracies can create hiring systems that take weeks or months to implement. When speed and flexibility are required, libraries may turn to nonprofit partners to take on the hiring role. The flip side of this is job sustainability, which can be more secure through a government employer.

- **Sharing Social Services among Libraries:** We're just starting to see some examples of this. As hiring library social workers becomes more popular, smaller libraries or library systems without the need for their own full-time position may band together to share access to a social worker, or a state library might provide social workers with office hours at libraries across one or more regions.

- **Challenges of Partnerships and Shared Management:** Virtually any library social worker hire is going to involve multiple partners. Hiring managers should think about how much control they want over the social worker's daily work life and how much time they're willing to devote to the significant communication that's necessary to co-manage successfully along with an outside organization.

There are, of course, other logistics that managers need to take into consideration upon hire. Office space, e-mail setup, equipment provision (computers and phones), and IT support all become more complicated when the host organization and the actual workplace are two different entities. For example, a library with a closed staff network for internet access, partnered with a nonprofit that provides the social worker's laptop and e-mail account, may find the social worker can't log in and get access to internal shared library drives and intranet. We won't get into the weeds here—just make note that if you're hiring with one or more partners, you can't always rely on existing procedures to meet all the social worker's needs, so you'll have to think more thoroughly and plan more carefully than you would for a typical hire.

In addition to considering the pros and cons of various host organizations, libraries can choose to pursue a variety of funding options:

- **Grants** to fund a social worker on contract are a common next step for libraries in the process of demonstrating a need for full-time support. The Institute of Museum and Library Services (IMLS) is the primary source of federal grant support for libraries. In some cases, like Niles District Library's grant for a group of libraries in Southwest Michigan, the IMLS funds arrive via a state-managed Library Services and Technology Act (LSTA) grant ("SWiRSL" 2018). Grants can also come from private foundations, many of which have missions to address and alleviate poverty that dovetail with library social work. For example, Anchorage Public Library's social worker was initially funded by a local mental health foundation (Hatch 2017). The St. Paul Public Library's first social worker was funded by a combination of these options (Steiner 2018).

- **Library foundations or friends groups** are another option, though usually only in larger library systems. Social workers in Seattle Public Library and in the King County Library System in Washington are funded at least in part via their library foundations ("New Community Resource Specialist— The Seattle Public Library Foundation" 2018; Box 2017). This funding is similar to grants in that it likely requires careful documentation and may have a limited timeline, though with greater possibility of renewal and sustainability over time.

- **Existing library FTE** can be a good long-term option, though it too is often initially offered for just a year or two to test the position's viability. Creating and funding a permanent position obviously requires support, advocacy, and flexibility at the highest administrative levels. However, it's not always necessary to add FTE to existing staff in order to bring a social worker on board. Some systems hire people with social work backgrounds into existing library staff positions. Jason's boss in Kansas City was one such hire as an outreach manager. Another example is Ursula, who applied for a library job even though she had no library background and has since flourished by adapting her social work skills to library administration. One challenge of funding this way is balancing the requirements of the preexisting job with evolution to include social work skills.

- **Budget lines from other government agencies** require a lot of negotiation and political relationship-building but may be one of the most sustainable options in the long run. Local social service departments in the United States receive funding specifically earmarked for the type of outreach work library social workers do. A natural next step from contracts may be for departments to take on greater collaboration and find ways to incorporate existing services into libraries. The Free Library of Philadelphia is one system placing social workers in libraries through a city partnership ("National Social Work Month" 2015). Delaware offers a similar example: its state library system has placed a roving social worker at several library branches in partnership with its state's Department of Health and Social Services ("Pilot Program Will Connect Library Patrons to State Services" 2018). As we go to print, the Delaware program will be expanding to all public libraries across the state.

Finally, it's always possible to find a unique source of funding you can adapt to your needs. Devon, director of a suburban public library, shared,

> We are really fortunate in the state of Massachusetts to have something called state aid. The state provides money to all libraries who are certified with Massachusetts Board of Library Commissioner, that is allocated based on demographic and other data, and that money can be used for any "library related purpose." That is going to enable us to use those funds to do this pilot. Our hope is that we will track the number of referrals and interventions and that we will utilize the data to make a case to have this position funded by the city beginning the following year and ideally to expand it from a part-time to a full-time position.

Check with your state library association or regional library network to see whether there are funds available for special projects, and keep an open mind about how you can utilize any extra funding, even if it's not specifically marked for this type of opportunity.

Data Collection and Documentation

As we saw in Ashley's example, it's crucial to continue to collect data and document impact throughout the life cycle of a library social work hire, not only for funders but also as a way to better understand your community and what adjustments you can make to best serve their needs. Earlier in this chapter, we shared examples of library social worker hires based on data collection. Kai, a librarian, experienced a similar success using data to request permanent funding:

> I think folks really appreciate the value of the service, and we were kind of pleasantly surprised how easy it was to convince the mayor's office to add this to the budget for next year. But I do think part of it is [that] before we made the proposal to even do this, we did a lot of tracking of different kinds of questions that the library was getting, and we've measured outcomes really carefully in a lot of different ways, so we were able to present a case for why this was important, what the impact was that were having for our patrons and for the library overall, and so I think that that really helped in terms of getting those municipal funds.

The same kind of information Kai collected can be used for everything from grant reporting to justifying the move from a contract position to a permanent hire.

Social Service Data Collection

Librarians and social workers each have specific data requirements and differing traditions of data collection. For both professions, our data collection priorities are grounded in our professional ethics, discussed in the introduction. It's helpful to have a basic understanding of these differences when you and your partners start collaborating because it can save you from some misunderstandings down the road.

In both academic and public libraries, staff take the library's commitment to patron privacy seriously. Librarians like the Connecticut Four, who went to court to refuse to comply with PATRIOT Act demands for patron information in the early 2000s, have earned libraries the right *not* to collect and save borrowing and computer use histories (Goodman and Goodman 2008). Because libraries don't ask unnecessary personal questions, they may have little idea of the racial makeup of library users, for example—or if they do, it only applies to attendees at specific programs who choose to complete evaluation forms. When libraries do collect information beyond numbers and program-specific information, it often takes the form of personal narratives or testimonials from patrons. Because protecting patron privacy is such a strong value throughout librarianship, library staff can feel daunted or even threatened by the amount of data social workers regularly collect.

Social workers often have an opposite problem to librarians. Rather than feeling restricted in the kinds of data they can collect, they face a wealth of information, the access to which can have very real legal, personal, or professional consequences. Before social workers can make a recommendation, design an intervention, or determine the status of a case, they have to assess and record as much data as possible. This might include a person's name, address (current and previous), phone number, employment status, employment record, age, race, gender, income, marital status, parenting status, name of parents, name of children, name of siblings, name of partners, name of friends, educational background, school attendance record, grades, criminal record, I.Q., developmental level, mental health status, medical diagnoses, use of alcohol, use of cigarettes, health insurance, personal life goals, and more. Social workers go to the trouble of collecting all this information because of their core professional commitment to serving the whole person.

Collecting this data serves multiple purposes. It helps the social worker remember information while developing a relationship with a client, and later it may be needed to justify decisions about the frequency, type, and intensity of social services chosen for the client. Social workers also collect data because their jobs depend on it. Many social workers are paid with revenue generated through health insurance plans, federal or state government contracts, or grant funding. That funding can continue only as long as social workers can prove their services are necessary. Finally, social workers are often called upon to testify in court on a number of matters, such as child or elder abuse determinations, custody disputes, mental health assessments, drug or alcohol treatment, appointment of guardianship for vulnerable adults, and restitution to victims of crime, all of which may require evidence that can be provided only through extensive data collection.

Social workers who are baffled by the limitations of library data collection should be aware that even the participation numbers that libraries collect can have a huge impact at the macro level. Use statistics demonstrate that need exists in the community. In combination with demographic data on rates of poverty, homelessness, and mental health and substance abuse issues, those simple head counts can provide a powerful initial data set for programs to establish their place with government systems and funders.

Librarians who may be concerned about collecting so much private patron information should know library social workers can't and shouldn't share confidential information with library staff. Social workers can, however, use their access to this data to understand why patrons display certain behavior, why they keep coming to the library, and what services they've already accessed. This creates a context for addressing behavior and for giving the most accurate referrals to other agencies. It also gives the social worker a framework for developing targeted library staff trainings and skill-building services.

Collaboration and Data Sharing

Given that librarians collect far less information than social workers need, and social workers have more information than library staff would ever want to access, where have library-social work partners found common ground? The good news is our overlapping interests are substantial enough that there are plenty of examples. This section isn't meant to be a comprehensive guide to how to collect and assess program data but rather to present a few options with specific relevance to library social work. If you're looking for a starting point to learn about assessment, we recommend the introduction to outputs and outcomes offered by the Institute of Museum and Library Services. It and other specific websites and tools mentioned in this section can be found in this chapter's online resources.

Yusef found the Harwood method to be a useful structure for approaching community members and documenting their needs:

> Our [library's] executive director was the first administrator trained in the Harwood methodology, . . . and he was really vigilant about meeting with local municipality and other not-for-profits, and even the community over-all, to really figure out how to learn from the information he received,

utilizing the tools. There's all kind of tools within that Harwood methodology where you can extract and put away a lot of narratives from community members and key stakeholders about how they view the library, how they think the library could improve, some challenges, things they're concerned about, and we are really having a process where you can gather information and data to make sure or validate the reasoning for having a social worker. So that means speaking with people experiencing homelessness, living in poverty, other service providers, and [other people] in the community as well.

The Harwood methods are supported by the Public Library Association (PLA) and have ranged from free online resources to conference sessions and training institutes, so libraries that are interested in the model can scale their use to their budgets. These tools engage the community in meaningful conversation about the direction of the library and its role in society.

Another PLA resource is Project Outcome, which includes instructional materials and assessment tools. Many of the surveys in Project Outcome are pre-made for specific types of programs, with the community engagement template likely the most useful for social service–involved programs. Libraries can start using the ready-made tools right away, but they can also dig much deeper into methodology through the robust series of instructional videos and guides. Topics include designing your own outcomes and outcomes-based questions, interpreting data, creating reports for sharing, and more. Registered libraries are also able to compare their results to other libraries throughout the nation. Data from Project Outcome, along with stories collected through Harwood tools, can combine to create a complex and useful picture of community demographics and needs.

Regardless of whether your library uses Project Outcome or your own surveys, the results can be almost immediately useful. Vivian said, "We recently did a survey, and 27% of our regular users have experienced homelessness in the past year, and so we wanted to bring someone in that can help a little bit more with those resources. We're a very busy library, and we were having trouble determining what people needed help with first because people's issues can be very complex. So, we have some interns who come in, . . . and we're working on a grant for a full-time social worker." We learned later that their grant application was successful based on Vivian's data collection.

Survey results can also yield information you might not expect. As Kai explained, "One of the interesting things we've found . . . is that because we sometimes survey folks who aren't using the service [of a social worker in the library] but are also maybe low income or are experiencing homelessness, and even for folks who aren't using the service and don't plan to use it really, it gives them a much more positive perception of the library." Kai also mentioned that "the other thing that we've been tracking is that staff feel much more supported," alluding to the results of surveying staff members as well as patrons. This is a great way to find out where social workers should start upon hire, as well as get feedback over time for continuous improvement. Surveying staff for their own social service–related patron interactions can harvest a wealth of useful data, along with stories to explain the limits of what library staff members are able to do on their own.

Finally, as social workers become more established in libraries, they are beginning to develop their own hybrid techniques for data collection. Evy, a social worker in a suburban library system, calls her library's technique collecting "mini-case studies," with not as much detail as the typical intake form but enough for her social work team to make appropriate referrals. A sample intake form is included in appendix D and as a document in our online resources that can be downloaded and edited for your library's needs.

Onboarding

Perhaps the most important finding in our work is that in the rush to hire a social worker, libraries and partners often don't plan for the transition staff and the social worker have to make, or for the supports that will sustain the social worker as a professional. A few years ago, this made more sense, given that very few people had been through such a transition. Now, collectively, libraries have enough evidence available to plan ahead and build the infrastructure needed to make these collaborations a success.

Roles and Communication

One of the universal challenges library administrators face is defining and communicating the new social worker's role. Both library staff and the new social worker should feel secure and able to explain how changing roles and responsibilities relate to the existing staffing structure. Some library staff may not know what a social worker does, and referring back to chapter 1 can help provide a basic explanation and resources. But the main challenges lie in the expectations people develop based on their understanding of current workflow and how those expectations are managed by everyone involved.

Before bringing a social worker on board, library staff and administrators may have grown used to doing their own crisis management for patrons, even if they lacked support or training. The initial relief library staff feel at having a social worker on board may create unrealistic expectations for change. Vivian explained, "The challenge we had [was] I think staff thought that as soon as we brought in a social worker, incidents at our library would drop off immediately. And the social worker could help with current incidents, but a social service person can't help if someone is currently intoxicated and throwing punches. That's not something they can help with. So, training staff was a bit of a challenge, but I think we're all on the same page now."

Vivian's experience touches on how a social worker's role can overlap with staff in a variety of positions in the library. They manage some crises for which staff may have called security or police in the past. They greet patrons and answer questions similar to frontline staff. They make decisions and give training on a new vision for the library, alongside administrators. Because these areas of overlap are so often in flux, it's important to foster collaboration and communication among everyone involved. Bradley said it was critical to "work with staff to define roles. I think part of that was the integration of a whole new model of social work, trying to figure out what the roles are, and we address that with training and things of that nature, giving people tools, in my department and outside to equip themselves to be able to engage in a higher level but really making sure that we are sending the message that we all work together."

Preparing staff members for their roles and the role of the new social worker can also help manage patron expectations. In reflecting on his experience, Yusef said,

> A lot of [my work] has been time and understanding, trying to get library staff to understand what exactly it is we do, but also I think there's a lot of relief, a lot of the staff finally have people around that could help with people they have been seeing for years, so there's a tendency [for staff] to over-promise at times. . . . So [a patron] will come in assuming that they will be getting a shelter plus housing subsidy or something to that effect because the librarian had told them that, so there is a little of that that goes on.

Being realistic about what the social worker can and cannot do in their position within the library will help to prevent confusion, frustration, and disappointment when problem situations don't immediately get better, or when they require different responses from library staff than they are accustomed to giving. On the flip side, library managers should be prepared for the social worker to spend time at the start of their appointment attending to these role distinctions and mediating between staff and administration. One good way to gauge initial staff knowledge as well as the social worker's impact over time is a periodic staff survey, an example of which is included in appendix E and online.

'Sustained communication about roles and responsibilities extends to partners as well as library staff. We touched on some of this in the section on differences in librarian and social work data practices, but it extends to other elements of work culture as well. Anya is a library social worker who is employed by a health care provider. In order to try and pay for Anya's positions, the health care company wanted to bill patrons for the social work services Anya was offering. In exploring this possibility, she said, "I have consulted with [other library social workers] to see if this was happening and brought it back to the [library] director, and she said, 'No, we shouldn't be billing for services.' That was a difficult thing to navigate in terms of this partnership and expectations and funding and everyone having different goals." While it makes sense a health care provider would want to bill for services, librarians will recognize immediately that doing so goes against the public library mission of providing free access for all, and in fact many public libraries are prohibited by law from charging for programs and services. The health care provider was acting in good faith from their common work practices and came up against a surprising conflict. Planning for ongoing communication at the administrative level could have saved Anya the stress of playing the role of go-between and bearer of bad news. There will be a lot of instances like this one in any collaboration, and it won't be possible to anticipate them all, but everyone involved can be psychologically prepared to handle them as they arise.

Special Considerations for Working with Youth

So far, most library social workers have been hired to work primarily with adults. Some systems, like St. Paul Public Library (Steiner 2018), are beginning to focus their social service efforts on youth under age 18, but all public library social workers should be prepared to encounter young folks. Anya has made time to attend to youth as well as the adults she typically serves: "I also work and spend time in the teen loft. Recently . . . they started up a [Gay-Straight Alliance] group there, and so I came and talked about stress management, and I have hours there, so teens can come and talk to me if they need a safe person to talk to [or] if there's a teen experiencing homelessness. I'm there to help guide them through that and contact the right people." This has been a positive experience for Anya, but not every library social worker has the background to attend immediately to the special needs of youth. Iris, a social worker with library office hours, encountered this and explained, "Youth [under 18] would come in that I didn't feel comfortable in working with, just because of how my position was set up. I was unfamiliar with the privacy rights and certain laws that have to do with youth, so there are just constant shifts in the population." A benefit and a pitfall of working in a place that attracts every type of person is that you can't always choose who needs your help, and even the most careful pre-hire planning may not reveal who the social worker will ultimately serve. Managers should be prepared to provide extra support to social workers serving youth. Minors aren't always legally empowered to speak for themselves, and they're subject to much heavier regulation than adults. Social workers also may not understand the unique role many libraries have as safe spaces that aren't staffed by mandated reporters. Youth services librarians, who are already familiar with working with young people in challenging situations, can be excellent peer mentors and guides for social workers who are new to the quirks of serving young people in a public library.

Boundary Setting

Along with communication around expectations and roles, education on things such as boundary setting, TIC, mental health, and community services can be key to helping librarians and social workers better understand each other. Some useful social work concepts for library service have been covered in preceding chapters, especially PIE in chapter 1. Having some common language and an awareness of the approach being used can facilitate a comfortable transition.

Setting good boundaries is important for all public services staff in the library, regardless of whether a social worker joins them, but we choose to mention it here because library staff members who have strong boundaries also support the new social worker's role. As we saw in Ashley's story, it's common for staff to turn to the social worker for support and guidance, which the social worker can find taxing on top of their existing responsibilities. As Frankie, a social work librarian, articulated, "It seems like even for the personal issues, people just really see you as the solver of all things. So it can be really stressful, and I think libraries have to be really mindful of how they do it and how they inform their system and [set] expectations." Prior to implementing a library-social work collaboration, library systems need to consider how to meet the emotional needs of their staff. Strong boundaries help, especially in combination with reflective practice, which we'll explore in chapter 6.

Social workers understand they can't meet all the needs of the clients they serve. Their focus on empowerment and self-determination of the client means they can offer resources, guidance, and encouragement, but they can't guarantee a successful outcome. Librarians who have never been taught to set those boundaries in their services can easily feel obligated to help with personal issues and then burn out because they can never meet the unreasonable expectation to solve patrons' problems. Bella felt this acutely while she was working as a homelessness and poverty librarian: "I know it was a struggle for me all the time. I knew that I couldn't change everything, like I wasn't going to solve the problem, but it was still incredibly difficult to come into work and be confronted with those problems all the time and not feel like I wasn't doing enough. And I don't know how we can translate that sort of like social work idea of breaking it down into, 'okay, what is manageable, what can you affect, how can you affect change in this issue' for librarians as well."

Training, either from the social worker or from another social services expert, can help library staff set better boundaries, which in turn can help prevent burnout and help staff manage their part of a human services interaction before escalating to the social worker. In our own trainings, we make an analogy to reference services to put the librarian's role in the context of familiar work:

Setting boundaries: You're not responsible for the cookies!

Imagine someone comes to you at the reference desk and wants to learn how to bake cookies. It's something they've never done before. You might take them to the cookbook section or help them find instructional videos on YouTube, but ultimately they go home and try it on their own, and you're not responsible for the results. It's much the same with human services interactions: you can connect people with resources and give them guidance on using them, but what they do next isn't your responsibility.

We acknowledge that this is easier said than done. Cookies are one thing, but a person who needs a place to spend the night off the streets is quite another. This is where staff members' empathy for patrons can become a sense of obligation, and they may have a hard time letting go. Elana highlighted this when she said, "Part of our issue is educating some of our younger staff who are very enthusiastic and really think that they are social workers. . . . I try not to diminish people, but it's a very different skill set and educational experience." While some staff members will push themselves too far, others may need to be encouraged to see relationships as part of their reference collection. One safety net against extremes in either direction is making sure that frontline staff discuss and agree to the same general guidelines and to help each other uphold them. Administrators and managers need to buy into this and provide strong support, encouragement, and ongoing communication to facilitate this shift in library culture. Library staff at all levels should also be prepared for constant (re)negotiation of the boundaries they agree upon together. Relationship-based service is nourished through multiple conversations over time that create opportunities to evolve along with patron and staff needs.

Supporting the Social Worker

Quick-and-Dirty Library Education

We heard from several library social workers that they had to make more of an adjustment than they might have expected to library culture. It's easy for library staff who have been embedded in that world to take it for granted things function the way they do, but for the social worker, library norms are foreign and are often stumbled upon by chance. That's always going to happen to some extent—tacit knowledge and work culture are the hardest things to impart to any incoming staff. Still, providing some formal education about librarianship for social workers can help set the stage for success.

Some states provide introductory courses for incoming library staff that give a general introduction to library history and ethics and an overview of how libraries function. In Michigan, the SWiRSL team found this to be a useful introduction for their full-time social worker ("SWiRSL" 2018). Webjunction also offers free webinars on basic library concepts that can be customized to provide an introduction that is easy to incorporate into onboarding. Library social workers can benefit from attending local or national library conferences, and libraries will often write funding for such activities into their social worker project grants. Finally, if the hiring organization offers tuition reimbursement, social workers can benefit significantly from taking an introductory library and information sciences course. We have yet to see this implemented widely, but we expect as these collaborations become more established, formal education will not only be a way to give social workers a foundation in librarianship, but also eventually act as a means for aspiring library social workers to distinguish themselves to potential employers. Plenty of library schools, including online ones, enroll non-degree-seeking students, and the expense could be reduced if needed through auditing a course. One unique option we include in this chapter's online resources is the Library Information Technology certificate program through Minneapolis College, which is entirely online and includes a concentration in public services.

Supervision and Professional Connection

While inter-professional collaboration can be exciting and offer many benefits to library social workers, the fact is they're usually doing their work alone. This manifests in the potential overload of staff requests for help mentioned earlier, but it also means the social worker can't easily connect with peers. Gianna, a library social worker, explained, "A social worker needs support by other social workers and other agencies because it can be very isolating to be alone, as it was my first year here, and I know some people continue to have that happen, and it can be really hard, so libraries need to make sure that their social worker has social work clinical support outside of the library as well."

As we mentioned in chapter 3 and will explore more universally in chapter 6, social workers rely upon reflective supervision by other social workers to process difficult cases, explore new ideas, and ensure best practice. This support is particularly crucial for library social workers as they expand and define their roles, which is why it's sometimes a good choice to have an out-side organization employ the social worker. This is the model being imple-mented by Devon: "This social worker would have to be supervised by the local mental health agency, not by a librarian. And I spoke with some of the librarians who have employed social workers in their facility, and one of the things that they mentioned, their detriment was that the social worker was being supervised by a librarian with no background in social work, so obviously [that] is not a good situation." Anya's experience supports that kind of choice: "I think that's one benefit of contracting with an outside agency—I do feel like I have a supervisor. She is very open that I can call if something weird happens and just process [it]. So that is very nice."

Anya is also the social worker mentioned earlier in the chapter whose employer wanted to bill for services provided in the library, highlighting the need for good communication between partners. Frankie, who is employed by a nonprofit but works in the library, had a similar experience of finding herself in the middle:

> Supervision can be a big issue in library social work. . . . I have two supervisors—the one in the outreach services department who's a librar-ian, and the other one a social worker who's off-site through the agency that I work for. And so, it's kind of like you're being pulled, . . . like you are told different things by different people. And there's someone that understands social work practice, while the other person is more library-minded and focuses on our department. And so it can be really tricky as a contractor to feel like you are not isolated, and that you're still part of the library. But then there's that flexibility in being a contractor that you can kind of do whatever's within your social work values, and you're not officially employed at the libraries, so there's not that barrier to doing what you feel is best. So . . . it's hard to figure out what would be the best balance for that.

Ideally, understanding this type of situation will arise in the course of any partnership, the managers who plan the hire will think through how to han-dle conflicts without making the social worker into a go-between. This is important work breaking down professional silos, and the social workers at the heart of it need robust support from all sides.

Finally, we don't want to overlook the importance of connecting with peers as a source of support. As library social workers have started to find their place, they are reaching out to each other across the continent and help-ing mentor new workers. The community of practice e-mail list on the WPL website is one important way library social workers can connect. In fact, it's often the first place most of the established library social workers refer new hires to connect with peers. Informal meetings and more formal workshop presentations at conferences hosted by ALA, PLA, NASW, and CSWE, among others, are another way library social workers are coming together to learn from and support each other. Some of those organizations also contain nascent professional library-social work groups, as mentioned later in our conclusion. We try to crowdsource, capture, and track as many of these opportunities as possible on the WPL website. These connections are growing rapidly and will be explored as future directions in the conclusion of the book.

Online Resources

www.wholepersonlibrarianship.com/book/resources/chapter4

- Links to:
  - Library assessment resources
  - Educational resources for social workers to learn about librarianship
- Printable, editable sample library social work intake form (also see appendix D)
- Sample survey for library staff feedback on social services (also see appendix E)
- Additional resources provided by you and your colleagues

CHAPTER FIVE

Advocating for Change

With the social work program, we really needed to reach out to the different organizations and get them on board and constantly advocate for ourselves, to everyone who is asking about why we needed to be there. You know, it was a suburban library, like we mentioned before, and not everyone sees homelessness in the suburbs. So, that was where a lot of my macro and more big picture advocacy skills came to work.

—*Iris, library social worker*

Overview

Advocacy on behalf of clients is a core activity in social work, more so than in librarianship. Social workers in libraries are already putting their advocacy skills to use for patrons, and there's a lot to be learned from their experiences. Librarians are also advocates, and in this chapter, we hope to expand the scope of what library advocacy can mean by viewing what's possible through a social work lens.

We begin this chapter by sharing the story of a library social worker who fostered self-advocacy for patrons experiencing homelessness. We will then explore the context of how social workers learn to advocate and how this differs from, but doesn't contradict, the traditional library approach. Finally, we will share insights from other library social work professionals on the importance of advocacy to their work and how they've brought it into libraries.

Leslie's Story

Leslie is the homelessness outreach coordinator at the central urban library in a large system. Like many full-time library social service providers, Leslie is supported through an arrangement that grew from the overlapping interests and needs of the organizations: "A lot of entities are investing in try-ing to make services available to patrons who are coming to this library on a daily basis, likely not accessing services at other places, and really need sup-port to get back into housing and on benefits." Leslie is on contract[1] with a nonprofit organization, providing an array of services to people experiencing homelessness, but her primary workplace is the library.

Leslie had been working in social services for many years before starting at the library. Leslie's position is divided equally between providing direct patron support and strategic planning. Twice each week, she holds office hours for patrons who need assistance in finding housing, shelter, food, and other basic needs benefits. Each month, she sees approximately 150 patrons in the library. Most of the contact she has is patron-initiated: "There are folks who want to come here and have this be the place where they feel like a com-munity member and they're not being labeled. And so I try to allow people to use the space. And of course, I don't know whether someone needs help or whether anything I have might be useful to them. So I really try to let [the help I offer] be mostly led by the requests the patrons are making."

Leslie also receives referrals from security officers and library staff when they encounter patrons who might need assistance. For example, one morn-ing a patron entered the library without any shoes. The security officer approached the person and said patrons couldn't be in the library without shoes, but rather than kicking them out, directed them to Leslie for help. Leslie said the staff spend a lot of time tracking her down to help with regu-lar patrons: "You know the staff has a lot of eyes and ears on the floor, and they know their floors really well. So, they a lot of time keep me cued in if there's somebody that they're worried about, and I'll try to look for opportu-nities to connect with them."

Within her office hours, Leslie provides 15 minutes to each individual patron, one-on-one, to talk about their lives, learn what they need at the moment, and make referrals. Because the meetings are short, Leslie said she tries to "stay away from too much case management and refer people to more intensive case management." Leslie places relationship-building at the center of her work, both with patrons and with partners: "I have [someone] that I'll meet with this afternoon . . . who needs to get enrolled in medical insurance. So I just messaged this [health care] navigator, and she's coming over here to meet us. . . [I have] a lot of partnerships where I rely on the expertise of other folks." Those partnerships not only create pathways for patrons to access resources—they also provide context for Leslie's work so she understands and is grounded in the library's role when she engages in advocacy work.

---

1. As of early 2019, her position is fully funded by the county and has become permanent.

Advocacy work comes into play in the other half of Leslie's position, where she champions programming and policy development based on patron and staff input. A significant part of the work has been the formation of a homelessness advisory board. The relationships Leslie developed with patrons experiencing homelessness through her office hours and through participating in Coffee & Conversation (a program described in chapter 2) got her thinking about how to turn patron requests into direct action and change. The catalyst for the advisory board was a community organization that approached Leslie and asked how it could contribute funds in support of services to patrons experiencing homelessness. The resulting seed grant has since been supplemented with library foundation funding. Leslie said, "It wasn't just going to be lip service. We were going to listen to their requests and then actually have some money set aside do something." The grant also enabled Leslie to offer meals and gift cards to participants. Leslie felt fortunate that her system was able to offer compensation to the board members for their time and contributions but went on to say, "In the real world, some boards are paid and some boards are not paid. . . . I think offering tokens so people can get to the meeting and leave [or] offering a meal is a great way to [minimize] the impact, like not making somebody's days more challenging in order to come."

Prior to starting the advisory board, Leslie reached out to other organizations to discover how they had managed to put together groups of people impacted by homelessness. Her goal in developing the group was to not make assumptions about what patrons needed or wanted, but rather to "support . . . the right to have their own voices heard and not have me or someone else speak on behalf of them." She began by inviting patrons who she knew had experienced homelessness and made use of the library, "so they were really invested in how things at the library would work." Eventually, she developed a core group of approximately 12 people. Leslie and two of the library staff members would facilitate the meetings, but they were clear about their role and worked hard not to influence the direction of the group. The board settled on a few priority items and broke into groups to work on "programming, resources, building accessibility, and security stuff. And then systematically working those things and making formal requests to the library. At first, it was like dumping ideas about . . . 'I noticed this with security' and 'We don't have enough newspapers' and 'Why are there cameras in the bathroom.'. . . It's just this sort of purge. Because a lot of members said, 'No one has ever asked me what I need or what I see.' And so a lot of the comments that we got were just thank you for listening to me and caring." The support of the library system meant listening was not the only result but could become the first step to making real change.

The most successful initiative undertaken by the board was an effort to open the library atrium on Sunday mornings. Leslie reflected, "The group talked a lot about [how] on Sundays there aren't a lot of places they can go and access bathrooms and be sheltered from the elements. And the library doesn't open until noon, and the atrium is open at 11." The board made a formal request to the library administration and building management to discuss their proposal. They didn't just ask for the atrium to be opened earlier but wanted to use the time and space to "offer information, programming, [and other] things to do." Library management approved a four-month pilot, and according to Leslie, it's been a "huge success" and is still going strong over a year later. Leslie said she stopped by recently on a Sunday, and on that day alone, over 125 people had gone through "the programming space where we had chessboard and tabletop gaming and adult coloring books and some really mellow programming. [Sometimes] we show a movie . . . so folks can just come in and chill out." Now that the Sunday morning atrium project has proven to create such a safe and inviting space, the board is looking to expand the services and information offered.

Leslie said an integral part of the success of the atrium project has been the participation of "a number of [library] staff that had been involved in craft club and chess club and were doing those types of programming. And so those staff kind of rotate through. . . . I think most of them do one Sunday a month where they're generously giving up their desk time to come and make this space available by staffing it." Volunteers from the board have also been involved in helping to make the mornings successful: "Yesterday we had two of our advisory board members volunteer—brewing coffee all morning, setting out games, refilling the sugars, . . . giving their own time as well to help minimize the impact on library staff. . . . They went through the application process and the formal volunteer process. So they are true library volunteers, and so they are able to take on those responsibilities."

The board also provided feedback on other established programming, such as employment services. The librarian responsible for employment programming at the Central Library came to the board to ask for their perspective on job support services: what they needed, what barriers they saw, what was and wasn't going well. That conversation informed the development of a job search lab within the library. Leslie said the board has become an invaluable resource to the staff: "It wasn't like, 'We think that you need to add something like this,' but that the board, now that it's established and there's this great momentum, there is now a group that library staff can come to get feedback on ideas that they're already working on."

In addition to programming, the advisory board has taken on policy changes impacting patrons in the library. Leslie described a particularly contentious policy the board worked on regarding patrons who are found sleeping in the library. The original policy was that patrons who were found sleeping would be woken up by security staff. If this happened three times within a day, the person would be asked to leave the library for the day. The board wanted clarification on the policy as well as more consistency regarding enforcement of security procedures. One of the things the board asked was for library staff to be the ones waking up patrons, instead of the security officers. Leslie said, "We were able to pass on this message of, 'You know, actually patrons would rather have it be your friendly face than a badge coming up to them to wake them up.'" This was helpful to hear because many staff didn't think patrons wanted them involved in waking them up. Leslie recognized it was an important conversation to have, especially since it was coming directly from the patrons who were most impacted: "When you change a policy, you're forcing people to talk about why it is the way it is and why we might stand to change it. And I think those conversations help to inform and educate people. And so I think that's always really positive." Eventually the policy was modified so patrons were no longer asked to leave the library simply for sleeping. Patrons could still be woken up—especially if they were asleep in front of a computer or sprawled out on the floor, or security had a concern about their well-being—but they would no longer be asked to leave the premises.

Despite many successes, there have been challenges along the way. Leslie said of the group, "I tried really hard not to just pick people who I thought could articulate themselves well, or who met a certain profile." This meant board members brought all the same experiences and behaviors to the group as they did to life on the street, which could, at times, create friction. Board members worried about their reputation and whether everyone involved could "represent our group well." But including this wide range of experiences was important to Leslie, even when it was difficult: "We don't always get consensus, but that's good too because there isn't one singular voice that's saying, 'This is what we need, this is what the barriers are.' . . . We've got people coming from a lot of different places." When asked how the group ultimately made decisions, Leslie said, "Everybody's got to be like 80% okay with stuff. We're all going to make concessions. It [can be] like, 'We need this document done by the end of this meeting, so do you want this included in the proposal?' And if five [people] say no, we [say to them], can you live with it being in there? And they're like yes. So folks still disagree, but the group's been so respectful of one another, really accommodating." In keeping with their roles as facilitators, Leslie pointed out that "the staff and I do not have a vote. . . . I like to play devil's advocate a lot, . . . but then ultimately the vote is in the hands of the members."

Another challenge, which can also be viewed as a success, is the evolving life circumstances of those on the advisory board. Leslie explained, "One interesting thing that's happened which I think is cool and worth noting is that most of the members of the advisory board have become housed while they've been on the board. Which I think has to do in part with the momentum that you can get from feeling empowered. I think everyone was living in shelter or outside when they joined, . . . and now we have [only] one or two members left that are still without a place to live. And so that's really cool." However, this does mean Leslie has had to consider inviting new people onto the board in order to ensure the continuous representation of diverse voices of patrons who are currently experiencing homelessness.

Inviting new members has led to some discussion and debate within the board as they have tried to determine criteria. Leslie started the group by mining her own relationships with patrons. Now that it has become a more established group, people interested in joining the board have to fill out an application. Developing this application required the group to discuss what questions and information were most important. Leslie explained,

> We had conversations in our meeting about what kind of questions we want to ask, what's important to us. And so we're asking questions about, "What has your personal experience with homelessness been? Where are you staying right now? What kinds of things do you use at the library? What do you wish the library had more of?" But really trying to be more thoughtful about who we invite and how being able to join the advisory board is a cool opportunity for people, and we don't want it to be about who you know, where you get in if you know somebody.

The formalization of the process and inviting new members has also led to conversations about sustainability of the board. The group is trying to decide what it will focus on next or whether the board should wrap up after one more large effort. Leslie says the relationships built on the board have been incredibly rich and important to the members, and "no one in the advisory board wants to leave. We have this really solid group that has become friends and have gotten to rely on each other, and they're so consistent about coming. . . . It's really impressive." Leslie thinks the board may disintegrate for a time but then come back as needed, "the same as you would do with a strategic plan, where you would keep coming back and revisiting it, . . . so build up some momentum and then let those programs work for a while, and then come back to it periodically." Until that next round of change is needed, current members and future patrons can continue to participate as official volunteers at the Sunday morning atrium programs.

Leslie acknowledged how important the support of upper-level management and administration has been to the board's success: "The support that we've gotten at the library has been amazing. . . . I have been so impressed, and as I compare with other library systems, they're not getting as much support as we're getting." This support extended beyond patrons to library staff and security officers. Leslie has observed staff becoming more interested in the needs of patrons, especially those who may have had "preconceived notions about things that they find upsetting about the way the patrons behave. Oftentimes, when they learn a little bit more about why certain behaviors are happening, . . . instead of being like, 'Oh my god, did you know that that guy charged the officer?' They [might say], 'Oh, I didn't know he was having a bad day, I wish I would've talked to him, and maybe I could've redirected him.'"

When asked what was coming up next for Leslie and her work, she said board members are interested in developing a program called "Homeless 101" for people experiencing homelessness for the first time. "A lot of the members reflect back on the days or the weeks that they had first entered into shelter or began sleeping on the train or outside. And it feels like they really didn't know where to turn, and for many of our members the library is the place that they went to. You know, it's like, if you don't know where to turn, start at the library because they'll have something, right?" Leslie believes no matter what comes next, in order for any program to be as effective as possible, she and the rest of the library staff must continue to listen to patrons: "There's so much to benefit and improve and enhance the services that the library is doing by getting feedback from the people that we're targeting those services to. All it can really do is help improve the efforts that the library is already doing."

Advocacy through a Social Work Lens

Social work is one of the few professions in which advocacy is not just a value, but a job requirement. Social workers are trained in political advocacy, policy development, community organizing, and civic engagement. The NASW Code of Ethics mandates social workers "advocate for living conditions conducive to the fulfillment of basic human needs and should promote social, economic, political, and cultural values and institutions that are compatible with the realization of social justice" (NASW 2018). This gives social workers the ability and authority to represent the rights of their clients and to engage in politics in a way few other professions can. Social workers place relationships at the center of their work and listen to clients and partners in order to discern what will be most helpful to them. They grow their advocacy expertise by learning to recognize common interests, frame sensitive issues, and navigate political systems and procedures.

Where social workers feel compelled to speak on behalf of vulnerable clients and populations, librarians can sometimes feel blocked by the value of professional "neutrality." ALA's Code of Ethics states librarians should "distinguish between our personal convictions and professional duties and . . . not allow our personal beliefs to interfere with fair representation of the aims of our institutions or the provision of access to their information resources" (ALA 2017). Interpretations of how exactly this should play out in libraries and whether libraries can even be "neutral" are well documented through decades of professional disagreement. Ursula, who spent a lot of time studying library history and ALA policies for her library position, uses a social justice-informed approach: "I have heard librarians say to me or to others libraries are neutral places, and that is not accurate. If you look at the history of libraries, libraries have always taken a very strong stance when it comes to social justice. It has always been like that." We raise the issue here because we know it will come up for librarians who may feel cautious based on a perception that advocacy requires them to choose a political stance and therefore show public bias to patrons. However, the social work approach sees advocacy not in terms of political sides but in terms of the best interests of the client and what will best promote equity across all types of people. Adopting a social work approach calls on library staff to ground themselves in the best interests of patrons as whole people, defined by what those patrons share as experts on their own lives. Rather than imagine they can keep their personal beliefs out of these interactions, social workers maintain constant self-awareness and transparency with the hope of identifying and counterbalancing any biases they bring to the table. We'll explore this approach more extensively in the chapter 6 discussion on reflective practice and cultural humility.

Social workers believe the people most involved in whatever issue is at stake should be empowered to act on their own behalf. This is why Leslie's first choice to make the library better for patrons experiencing homelessness was to give them the option to speak for themselves. Yusef, a social worker, also stressed the importance of this type of inclusion: "We are really intentional about making sure that community-wide . . . decisions aren't being made without [including the] people receiving services. I have been at many meetings which are theoretical exercises at best. How does it work in practice? How do we implement many things of that nature? I think that the people we advocate for have just as much of a voice, if not more, in helping with how to provide the best services." In support of empowerment, the social worker's role is to use their knowledge of and place within systems of power to elevate the voices of the people they serve. Yusef did this by consistently consulting with patrons about high-level ideas. Leslie did this by creating a structure that would bring the voices of patrons experiencing homelessness into library policymaking and program design.

Leslie's advisory group was formal and funded. They were lucky to receive a small, relatively unrestricted grant to support their activities. One of the key factors to take into account if you have access to funding to assemble a group of people who are experiencing poverty or homelessness is whether and how to compensate their time. People who live in day-to-day survival mode may not have the capacity to give freely and expect nothing in return.

Compensation is a way to demonstrate their time is valuable, not only to the library but as the kind of expertise that should be paid. However, as Leslie noted, many advisory boards in the population at large are made up of unpaid volunteers. She also recognized, when considering whether this could be replicated in other systems, that funding isn't necessary: "We certainly want to be thoughtful about not taking advantage or making an assumption that, well you have nothing to do anyway, so just come and talk to us. . . . But I would like to leave the door open that if for whatever reason, a library system didn't have the ability to do that, there are ways to be creative about compensating people."

The balance Leslie struck—providing transportation assistance, meals, and gift cards—is a good demonstration of the fact that libraries don't need to have a lot of money in order to offer an incentive for participation. Nourishment is always welcome, so something as simple as a Coffee & Conversation group could become a de facto advisory committee if given enough time and trust. Transportation support can mean the difference between someone's ability to be present or not, so a handful of bus tokens can go a long way. Yusef didn't say whether he had a formal structure in place for consulting members of his community, but his and Leslie's experiences both point to the key factor at the heart of advocacy work: solid relationship-building over time, with multiple community members.

When it's not feasible to create a path for people to speak for themselves, social workers can and do step in and speak on behalf of the needs they perceive in their communities. This is where macro expertise also becomes especially important. Social workers—and librarians!—are sometimes able to see the whole picture, or the whole PIE, in a way people mired in their own struggles are not. Witnessing similar problems experienced by multiple individuals can indicate an issue with structural conditions, not individual fallibility, which many in society attribute to common social problems. Librarians and social workers, simply by virtue of their job roles, have power and privilege that goes beyond the reach of many patrons. In addition to examples mentioned earlier, librarians and social workers may have time and even employer support to go speak to a state senator or city council, whereas someone working two or three jobs and single-parenting just wouldn't be able to fit it into their schedule.

Internal and External Advocacy

There are two main avenues for advocacy alongside or on behalf of patrons. Internal advocacy happens within our organizations to change policies and procedures. This is where Leslie's group had its major successes. External advocacy involves speaking up outside of the workplace to better our patrons'

lives and tends to be where we encounter more pushback to remain profes-
sionally "neutral," or at the very least to be politically disengaged. However, a
social work perspective reminds us we can be political on behalf of the needs
of our patrons without being partisan. As library systems become more influ-
enced by corporate norms, which center the needs of the organization over
individuals who make up the organization, they adopt the expectation
employees will only advocate publicly where the library system has taken an
official position. Social workers experience these challenges, too. They're
often employed by government entities and can feel constrained by their
employer when it comes to championing the best interests of their clients.

This tension among the employer's party line, patron needs, and staff
beliefs about how best to proceed can't ever be fully resolved. Each situation
calls for a new navigation that takes everyone involved into consideration.
First and foremost, examine your position within your organization. Where
do you have power to affect the greatest positive change for your patrons? Are
you more comfortable influencing staff culture or public policy? How much
are you willing to risk your personal comfort to press for the evolution you
believe in? It's acceptable and even healthy protection against burnout to be
thoughtful about how, when, and where you invest your energy as an advocate. Your abilities and the needs of your patrons will also change over time,
so it can be helpful to check in with yourself periodically using a tool like
reflective practice, which we present in the next chapter.

Internal Advocacy

Librarians practice internal advocacy all the time by using a patron-
centered justification for revising library policies, regardless of whether
they're framing it in those terms. For example, in recent years, many public
and academic library systems have been going fine-free, based on the understanding that a punitive approach doesn't foster positive relationships
between staff and patrons (Miller 2018). Just like Leslie's group began by
addressing sleeping in the library, revision of library policies is a common
starting point for response to patron needs. Another approach can be refram-
ing policies as a patron bill of rights, rather than as a list of prohibited activities. Many existing policies are the legacy of a time when libraries thought of
their institutional needs ahead of patron needs, and updating them can be a
relatively speedy way to demonstrate responsiveness. A new policy structure
can also be a solid support for beginning a cultural shift in the library since
it provides concrete behavioral guidance for both staff and patrons. Examples from library systems that have enacted a patron bill of rights can easily
be found online and serve as guides to what others have found feasible.

Examining current policies and exploring new ones is a great activity for a student intern. Alecia, a medical social worker who completed her practicum in a library, explained,

> The library that I was at did require proof of address to use a library card. I just did a quick search of the homeless shelters in our [city] that let people use their address as a mailing address. I just typed that into [the librarian's] computer to see how many people had that address, and over 100 people have that shelter listed as their address and without the name of the shelter. So that was proof that people who are experiencing homelessness were using the library and were just kind of going under the radar because they did not look like someone that was experiencing homelessness.

Alecia was able to use that information to change the policy about proof of address at her library. She also said, "Another policy that the library had . . . was asking people to leave if they had an odor, which again is not unique. . . . I was able to get shower tickets to the swim center next door, and they donated a huge stack of them, about 500, and they were the same tickets that anyone else would use who paid for the swim center showers, so you wouldn't be identified, your ticket wouldn't be a different color just because yours was free." She got those tickets because of the community relationships she had built, but the challenge came with internal change: "I think what was hard was coming up with a policy of how this would be distributed, just because telling someone that their body odor is offensive is extremely difficult to approach. But I gave those tickets to whoever needed them, whoever said that they were living out of their car and didn't have a shower. I wasn't stingy with the tickets." This required agreement from her supervisors and established a far more positive approach than expelling patrons from the library.

Internal advocacy can also be a tool for shifting workplace culture alongside patron policy changes. Frankie, a social worker in a large urban library system, spoke of the importance of advocating for administrative support around TIC: "The bigger picture of trauma-informed care that I see the benefit of is it's an organizational commitment, . . . not only in policy, behavioral expectations of patrons and staff, but in training. So it's not just providing a one-off training here and there, it's really an embraced concept, . . . and the administrative policy supports it. Administrators support it. Our board of directors also understands what it is and what it means for the library and the services that we provide, that is the ultimate bigger picture." Frankie applied a PIE perspective to her workplace, which helped her see and explain that TIC wouldn't be sustainable without buy-in at all levels. This "next level" of internal advocacy takes more time and energy than any single policy shift but creates more sustainable change.

A different approach to internal advocacy is advocacy on behalf of colleagues. The ALA Code of Ethics includes this point: "We treat co-workers and other colleagues with respect, fairness, and good faith, and advocate conditions of employment that safeguard the rights and welfare of all employees of our institutions" (ALA 2017). The classic example of this is unions advocating for the rights of members, and many librarians are unionized and could bring a social work lens to any union involvement in which they choose to engage. However, one area where social work skills have yet to be fully explored for internal advocacy is within the hierarchy of management. A supervisor who uses a social work approach with subordinates listens carefully to their needs, believes them as experts on their own lives and work experiences, and then helps elevate their voices and supports the changes they request in much the same manner as a social worker with clients. Leah Esguerra uses this approach with supervision of her HASAs in San Francisco (see chapter 4), and she intentionally builds in time to every one of their shifts to listen and respond to their experiences. This is a form of reflective supervision, and it also serves the purpose of making Leah an informed advocate for her employees. There are many other ways social work skills can be applied to management, a topic we make note of in the conclusion for future exploration. Advocacy for employees is a natural extension of the approach social workers are already bringing to library settings.

Advocacy can also be internal to our professional organizations, the results of which can be a catalyst for change throughout libraries. For example, in 2018, members of the Gay, Lesbian, Bisexual, and Transgender Round Table (GLBTRT) successfully advocated for the ALA Council (the elected, governing body of ALA) to adopt a resolution in support of providing gender-neutral bathrooms at all ALA conferences (Ford 2018b). This was done at least in part to "[lead] the way as a model of inclusiveness for our libraries, many of whom do not offer gender neutral bathrooms" ("Selection of Resolutions Adopted by the ALA Council" 2018). This type of internal lobbying isn't new to librarianship, but it does take on greater meaning within the holistic approach provided by social work. It's an example of the leadership librarians already provide as advocates for each other, which can then be extended to the well-being of all library patrons. Implementing gender-neutral bathrooms in libraries is one of the tasks currently being tackled by many library social workers, and the successful advocacy provided by librarians within ALA creates a foundation social workers can in turn use for advocacy within their own library systems.

Internal advocacy has an especially nuanced role in academic libraries seeking to connect students with social services. As noted in chapter 2, academic librarians and other staff may be discouraged from looking outside of their own institutions to build community connections. Hester, who has master's degrees in both librarianship and social work, explained how she saw "a huge challenge of getting people to actually see that there are issues that need to be addressed because it's easier to say we don't see anything because then we don't have to fix it. [I'm] coming from an academic institution . . . where most students on campus have access to mental health resources, but the mental health resources that they have access to shut down at five, so from five until the next morning, they have nothing." In response, Hester has observed "there are some within the libraries and librarians who don't want to address those issues because some feel powerless" after having been told by their administrators those issues aren't ones for the library to address. She also noted academic staff say "I'll write a report on and I'll do research on it" but don't end up moving from their research into advocacy. There is no doubt a great deal of work remains to be done, but academic librarians are increasingly realizing they have a uniquely holistic view of student experiences and needs and can help advocate for those in a way their more siloed colleagues cannot.

External Advocacy

Social workers believe policies and laws set by government at local, state, and national levels are important tools for addressing social problems. As professionals, they're expected to be well versed in how to influence government alongside and on behalf of clients and vulnerable populations. Social workers in micro- or mezzo-level positions may participate in organizing and amplifying the voices of their clients, while macro-level social workers fill positions as lobbyists, legislative aides, and nonprofit and government workers who interpret and implement policies once they've been codified. Mary was one of these full-time, macro-practice social workers before she became a professor, and her experience spanned many different forms of external advocacy. She started her social work career as a community outreach worker for a small, rural domestic violence agency but quickly discovered her desire to work farther "upstream" when she witnessed the impact of government policies on the ability of her clients to obtain meaningful services. Along with a friend from her MSW program, she went on to found her own lobbying and advocacy organization to help nonprofits and community groups bring their concerns to government and work toward change for their clients. After several years of serving clients on issues such as K–12 student support, restorative justice, quality early childhood programming, youth mentoring, and child welfare services, Mary shifted gears to work as a health and human services researcher in the Minnesota state senate. Her responsibilities there included analyzing hundreds of policy and budget bills every year; writing talking points, media releases, and fact sheets for dozens of state senators; and providing constituent services for any concern falling in the very broad spectrum of health and human services (e.g., health care, child welfare, public health, welfare, nursing homes, hospitals). Mary's social work education was the foundation of her ability to analyze and suggest solutions to complex social problems, and her social work experience gave her the skills to present people's stories so they were relevant and comprehensible to policymakers. As a professor, she continues to help others not involved or connected to the political system navigate through complicated policy and bureaucracy by teaching her students about her own practical experiences.

Library social workers are equipped to help libraries with their own advocacy. Alecia provided a great explanation of how patron needs can connect directly to external advocacy work. She said that with her patrons at the library,

> I felt like all I could do in that moment was listen and validate that experience and not really have anything that would be a solution to them. We would fill out the affordable housing applications with a two year wait list, and it was really defeating to know that was all I could offer. And that's the reality of social work in the library—yes, to offer resources and to point people in the right direction, but when resources are scarce, what do you do from there? . . . I really encouraged the library system that I was working with to advocate for those services in their city. I think that that was a challenge for the library, who almost didn't want to be involved in that way.

She was very aware of what she could contribute as a social worker and also the larger implications of what she learned: "That was another opportunity for me to educate people about the importance of advocacy and speaking up for people that they see in the library. . . . I don't think that my region is unique—across the country libraries are all in this same problem about funding and decision-making, and I really hope that librarians have a seat at the table in their own city."

Alecia touched on a significant barrier to library involvement in external advocacy: hesitation to speak for patrons in a way that could be seen as biased. Realistically, though, librarianship as a profession already provides fearless external advocacy on a handful of key issues. Libraries and their representatives protect intellectual freedom through nationwide activities like Banned Books Week, and locally through the conversations collection managers have all the time with patrons who challenge library materials. The ALA Washington Office supports access to information through ongoing lobbying for federal funding of LSTA grants that in turn fund broadband internet access for rural and tribal libraries. These and some other issues feel "safe" and get strong support because they're included in the ALA Code of Ethics. This tight focus means there are great organizational supports in place to sustain ongoing advocacy in these areas. In addition to the ALA Washington Office, which is empowered to support the resolutions passed by ALA Council, many state library associations pay lobbyists and train library staff to participate in lobbying efforts. EveryLibrary has grown into a nationwide nonprofit by coordinating advocacy efforts for embattled libraries across the United States. Librarians also consistently produce programming to engage patrons in the democratic process, from supporting immigrants who are studying for their citizenship tests, to participating in ALA's partnership with the Harwood Institute to offer carefully crafted civic conversations in public libraries. All of this reflects librarianship's professional strengths in organization and structured participation.

There's also one subset of library staff who practice advocacy on a regular basis: library administrators, who learn some of those skills as part of their ascent up the career ladder. Because of how they learn and are encouraged to apply it to a specific set of tasks, they may come to see advocacy as a function of management, limited to the people in charge and the bureaucratic decisions that regularly bring them in front of a library board or city council. This reflects the fact that librarianship as a whole is missing the connective tissue between advocating for particular ideas, as opposed to the social work perspective of advocacy as a function of service. Librarians may be taught to fight tirelessly for a short list of values, but they don't learn a process of generating, selecting, and shaping patron stories to support concerns as they arise in their communities. Changes to library education standards can take a long time, but in the meantime, librarians can take advantage of the expertise of the growing number of social workers in their midst.

One example of how libraries can use a social work approach to become agents of positive change comes from contrasting stories presented by two of our interview participants. Both were public library administrators who faced negative feedback about the presence of patrons experiencing homelessness in the library. Owen defined it as "the subtle pushback that we get from the community as a whole. It's the mom who may mention something to one of her county commissioners that she was bringing her three-year-old daughter in, and they had to walk past some people that were fairly shabby while they were there. A policeman had to come in and escort someone out. It's not a real positive experience for the rest of our patrons, and it's a concern we have because taxpayers [are] our bread and butter." He took the responses of his patrons to heart, but he determined, "We are not promoting bringing social workers in to advocate for populations of those that are disadvantaged. Currently we have to call the police for drunks in the library. We have to go to police for mental illness. . . . I think social work intake has its place, but I'm not sure if the public library is exactly the most appropriate place for it."

In contrast, Ursula proactively used her social work skills to create an opportunity for social justice education. She said,

One of the things that we were encountering in the old town branch was a higher number of people without homes coming to spend time at the library, and we had patrons who didn't want them there. So what I offered the manager was, why don't we do a program that breaks down some of the myths that people have about people experiencing homelessness. . . . We created this focus group who worked to befriend shelters here in the community, and then we did one-on-one interviews with the people that wanted to participate, and we had a photographer, and we explained what we were doing this for and the intention behind it. . . . At the end, we created this exhibition at a place in the community that had beautiful pictures and quotes about [the meaning of] home, and it was just really beautifully portrayed. . . . One of the things that people said [in response] was that it was really hard to walk downtown seeing restaurants providing water for dogs but no water for people, so we put a dog bowl with water on top of a display of non-accessible water bottles. . . . [It became] an exhibition that you can pack and take other places, so we did that, and the exhibition was super successful.

Both Owen and Ursula acted in what they thought were the best interests of their communities as a whole. Owen's approach prioritized the voices of community members with the most power. Ursula, a social worker by background, immediately saw an opportunity to advocate for the rights of patrons who have the least social advantage and the most to gain from regular, welcoming access to the library. Her approach didn't reject the people who criticized the presence of patrons experiencing homelessness but rather sought to creatively inform them of things they might not know. Libraries considering whether this type of approach can work for them may appreciate her observation that they can "really capitalize on how much the community trusts the public library." She used that trust as a starting point to create more trust, rather than spending it down like it's a finite resource:

> I have been able to bring into the library conversation that people are afraid to have at any other place. Last year when we had the awful shootings in Orlando and police brutality on the TV, there was so much stuff going on, and people were really afraid, and we were having hard conversations here. I just sent an email to people in the community and said, let's have a conversation of how can we move the needle in social justice. We had people like the mayor, council members, the director of United Way, people from the school district, just sitting down at the library talking.

Ursula's experiences demonstrate, too, that advocacy doesn't always mean a loud voice shouting down the room. It can be conversation and the simple recognition of truths as observed within the safe space of the library.

Online Resources

www.wholepersonlibrarianship.com/book/resources/chapter5

- Links to:
    - Library advocacy organizations and associations
    - Social work advocacy sites
    - Sign up for the ALA Washington Office newsletter
- Additional resources provided by you and your colleagues

CHAPTER SIX

Sustainable Practice

These folks went to library school, not social work school, and then they are thrown in a setting where they are getting asked really challenging questions, and I think people can get a little burned out. They see a lot here, they see a lot of suffering and long-term repeated substance abuse, and that is hard.
—Cyndi, social worker

Overview

Empathy without boundaries creates burnout. Empathy not structured by preparation, planning, and follow-up creates burnout. Empathy not supported by like-minded colleagues creates burnout. Social workers built their profession around empathy, and by necessity this also means they became experts on preparing for, preventing, and treating burnout. Library staff who take on a more relationship-based role may fear emotional and psychological burnout, and for good reason—they're often asked to manage complicated interactions for which they have no formal preparation. Libraries will not be successful in their relationship-based efforts in the long term unless they recognize staff are whole people as much as patrons are. Staff members need time and tools to grapple and come to terms with the challenging interactions they face every day on the job.

In this chapter, we dive into the social work methods that enable human service with minimal burnout. First, we share a story of a librarian who discovered how reflective practice could help her own staff members. Next, we set the context for the importance of these concepts by explaining why we choose "sustainable practice" over "self-care." We then move into the basics of two core social work concepts, reflective practice and cultural humility, and how those can be applied to library public service. These practices work in tandem with concepts previously mentioned in the book, such as PIE and boundary-setting, and round off a whole person staff approach to whole person patron services.

Karen's Story

Karen Kolb Peterson[1] is the public services manager at the George Latimer Central Library in downtown St. Paul. Karen has been with the library system for decades and currently supervises staff across professional and paraprofessional job classes. Over the years, Karen has been directly involved in a number of challenging situations with patrons and has also watched her staff members grapple with how to handle them. In response, she tries to offer support to her staff through reflective practice and intentional supervision, giving them time and space to discuss, think through, and learn from the various challenges they face in the library. Karen said she feels her approach has helped her staff "go into the situation feeling, not armed (because that sounds too confrontational), but at least equipped to make it turn out as well as it possibly could."

One way Karen was able to foster reflective practice and cultural humility among her staff was through a collaboration with the Saint Paul—Ramsey County Public Health department and a program called The Wakanheza Project (see online resources). Karen explained, "The premise of The Wakanheza Project is that you don't know the situation from which someone has come when they walk into your space. For example, you don't know if they were just involved in a domestic dispute. You don't know if they've just been foreclosed. You just don't know. What we have with them is this moment, and how do we make it as positive as we can?" Taking this approach has helped staff enter interactions with openness, intentionality, awareness, and willingness to learn from themselves and from others.

The collaboration and the training came at a time when St. Paul Public Library was building homework centers for K–12 students. Library staff established good relationships with the students, and libraries had become safe spaces where, as the children became more comfortable, they began to share very personal stories. Karen reflected, "While librarians are not court-mandated reporters [of child safety violations], we as human beings would hear these situations with kids and wonder what we could do." She also recognized library stereotypes might keep patrons from reaching out for help: "The stereotype about libraries is all we do is shush people all day and that our goal is to keep everything quiet. If you come in with a kid, that doesn't always happen exactly

---

1. Karen's story uses real names.

that way. So we were trying to be accepting of people as they are, as they come in, and that included families and children and all the messiness and activity they bring." Karen and other library managers decided to search for resources that would help staff members to cope as well as have better skills for interacting with patrons who have challenging life circumstances.

In that search, they came across The Wakanheza Project, which had been adopted by other government entities and organizations in the region. Ultimately, library administration was so impressed by the project's content that they made it a mandatory training for all staff. Karen said, "We were so taken with this as a way that we could change our public face, change the way we choose to be with our public, . . . so in the same way that [new staff] learn about how you submit your hours, and how you dress for work, The Wakanheza Project helped us to think about how we want to be present when we welcome people into the library."

Karen believes learning better "guest care" led to better staff self-care. Being able to say and believe staff tried their best has empowered them to let go of their discomfort sooner than they had in the past. This idea of self-care has been important with some of the younger clerical staff at the library, who, Karen explained, "most directly interface with the public." Female clerks are especially vulnerable to male patrons who frequently watch or talk to them in ways that can feel threatening. Karen has spent time coaching these staff members to take their own feelings seriously and tell other staff when these situations occur:

> I say to them, "If that made you feel uncomfortable, we need to do something about it." They assume they're being overly sensitive and question their responses. They think, "I'm 18, I'm nearly an adult, I should be able to handle this. That person didn't touch me. That person didn't use profane language. But I just felt kind of sleazy about the way that they were talking to me." What I've had to say to them is that they need to trust their gut because if someone is making you feel uncomfortable, they can make someone else feel uncomfortable. And tell me or your supervisor so that we can support you and address the behavior or the conversations that are making you uncomfortable. My job as your supervisor, as your supervisor's supervisor, is to make this a place where you feel safe at work. If that behavior makes you feel unsafe, somewhat threatened, uncomfortable, we need to address it.

Karen meets with all of her staff both individually and in groups to address widespread issues of concern. She believes it is critically important for staff to raise issues and support each other. She sees her role as a supervisor is to "hire the right people, make sure that they have the right training, get out of their way so that they can do good work, and be accessible." Karen truly believes people skills are the most essential quality: "I can teach someone how to use reference tools. I can teach them how to use the technology. I can't as easily, as readily, teach them to be aware of their surroundings, to look people in the eye, to greet them, to acknowledge them, to see them." These people skills are addressed by what staff learn through The Wakanheza Project, even if those takeaways aren't always obvious to staff right away. Karen shared, "Despite our best efforts, I had someone say to me one time that using The Wakanheza Project and trying to bring yourself back to being intentional about how you interact with people doesn't always work. It doesn't always go the way you hope that it will." Nevertheless, Karen asserted the model is ultimately useful because "at least as you're thinking back on what happened and how it could have gone better. You acknowledge that you gave it the best you had with what you knew in that given situation."

Karen added a new element to her supervisory style just a year ago that she "would not give up for anything. I wish I could say it was my idea. All I did was recognize a very good idea from staff. In a library that's open seven days a week and where staff is present only when we're open, grabbing time for staff meetings is difficult. But every Monday, staff report at 11:30 and we open the doors at noon." During that weekly half hour, Karen convenes the staff to discuss "activities downtown impacting staff or guests, announcements, processing incidents, or issues that came up over the weekend. They may need to talk with their peers about a guest's behavior or a challenging situation. It might be introducing new staff. It might be talking about staff who are leaving. We talk about a replacement security guard who will be on site. I asked them to weigh in for me about issues and matters that impact them, and it's a check-in on all the things that I hope that they'll keep in mind." While she usually sees about half of her staff at these meetings, Karen also types up notes and sends them to everyone, "so whether they cared to come to the meeting, I feel like it's important that we share critical information about our work in this library."

Along with everything she and her staff learned from The Wakanheza Project, Karen believes this short, weekly meeting has changed the way business is done in the library. Staff are more connected to each other and the work of their colleagues. There is a greater sense of shared responsibility and community throughout the building. She concluded, "I think it's important we look each other in the face and talk about the things that we're proud of, worried about, thinking about—whatever it is."

Self-Care vs. Sustainable Practice

How many of us have read an article or Facebook post or even attended a workshop on self-care? It usually starts off with a litany of how hard we work, how difficult it can be, and how we can't help others until we help ourselves. We're told to "fill our cup" first before filling others, or there's a humorous quip about how you should "secure your own oxygen mask before assisting others." Then we're treated to an exhaustive (or exhausting?) list of all the ways we can take care of ourselves:

- Take a warm bubble bath
- Exercise every day
- Meditate every day
- Do yoga every day
- Journal before bed at night
- Drink wine
- Don't drink wine
- Spend time in nature
- Read a good book
- Spend time with friends
- Take a vacation
- Get eight hours of sleep
- Get nine hours of sleep
- Take a nap
- Eat well
- Cook
- Raise your own vegetables
- Eat more vegetables
- Drink eight glasses of water a day
- Avoid caffeine
- Avoid sugar
- Eat chocolate
- Avoid bread
- Eat whole grains
- Avoid meat
- Eat fish (but only certain kinds)
- Eat with your family at the dinner table every night
- Worship
- Volunteer

Mary is a good rule-follower and tried to incorporate as many of these as possible into her life, only to end up feeling like a failure. So she added up how much time it would take her to do all the self-care activities she thought she should be able to do, and it was an extra eight hours a day on top of work, sleep, and parenting. No wonder she didn't succeed! Self-care that becomes an additional obligation turns into self-defeat. We do believe self-care is important to remaining sane in daily life, but the problem with the preceding list is it puts all the responsibility for "care" on the individual. This becomes even more of a problem when work is emotionally and psychologically draining. Who makes space for us to do these things? Do they come more easily to people of certain incomes, genders, work structures, or socioeconomic status? Employers may encourage self-care, but if it's presented in the context of individual responsibility on personal time, that can end up compounding the problem. Employers in helping professions like social work and librarianship should be careful not to take advantage of their employees, who are likely self-motivated to do good work for others and therefore susceptible to taking on additional caring responsibilities at their own expense.

Sara knows several librarians who have quit their demanding public library jobs, reduced their work hours, or transferred because they burned out. There are many others like them out in the workforce who remain anecdotes but represent a collective need for a new approach to workplace support. Burnout is even more of a concern for people of color in librarianship, who deal with discrimination from patrons and the "responsibility" to educate colleagues (who are also suffering from a lack to time to process the things they need to learn in order to be good allies to their coworkers) on top of the same challenges their white or invisibly different colleagues face. In honor of this outstanding gap in workplace support, and in order to frame it as a professional necessity, we refer to structured self-care activities in the workplace as "sustainable practice." This shifts the responsibility of creating a culture that fosters quality service to the employer as well as the employee. Institutions, colleagues, and communities shape and support the employee experience as much as they do the patron experience, and the mental health of staff exists in symbiosis with the mandate to make everyone feel welcome in the library.

Cyndi, a social worker at an urban library, has seen firsthand how a lack of training in sustainable practice can lead to negativity. Her quote kicks off this chapter because it frames the issue of educational differences addressed here, but she first named the problem because she was "hearing some things [from library staff] that are shocking or that would never fly in social work school about the people we serve." Similarly, Ursula, a library administrator who has a social work background, observed library staff, "have the best intentions but never received training in how to handle difficult situations with people with mental health issues, or that people do not have homes, or domestic violence. We are seeing a high increase in drug abuse at one of our libraries right now, and they didn't go to school for that. . . . They never learned to deal with the stress associated with that or with just handling that patron, so you end up with librarians who are very frustrated from seeing behaviors that seem disruptive to them and to other patrons."

It's not the fault of library staff they didn't learn these skills in school—although that's something we call for as a next step in the process of collaboration between our professions—but it can be remedied through practical partnership with social workers. Karen's story provides one excellent example of how a community partnership, along with strong commitment from a library manager, can facilitate change. While having a social worker on site can create a shortcut to training on some of these methods, all library staff are capable of learning and implementing them.

Cultural Humility

Cultural humility is a term for how social workers and librarians approach people who come from all different backgrounds, while showing empathy and respect for each person's story. This hearkens back to chapter 1 because cultural humility describes how we approach what we learn from PIE: there are many factors influencing a person's life, and we can't know them all, but we can listen, trust, and understand that different experiences may lead people to different beliefs and behaviors from our own. The approach Karen learned through Wakanheza is grounded in cultural humility: "You don't know the situation from which someone has come when they walk into your space. . . . What we have with them is this moment, and how do we make it as positive as we can?" The individual approach advocated by social work, where each person is an expert on their own life, often happens as a micro-level interaction between individuals. Cultural humility is the macro-level version of that same idea.

The term "cultural humility" was coined in the 1990s by two nurse practitioners, Melanie Tervalon and Jann Murray-García, working in Los Angeles hospitals. Both women had witnessed the racial strife and pain that erupted following the "not guilty" verdict in 1992 of two white police officers for the assault of Rodney King, a black man whose beating was one of the first acts of racialized police violence to be recorded on video and shared widely by the media. Despite the growing popularity of "diversity training" in workplaces across the United States, and especially in Los Angeles, the nurses didn't see an improvement in how their colleagues related to patients from different racial backgrounds than their own. The Rodney King verdict sparked especially negative effects for patients of color being treated in hospitals and medical clinics. Tervalon and Murray-García (1998) hypothesized diversity training wasn't working because it was based on "cultural competence," which treated cultural knowledge as a checklist of items a person could complete once and walk away from feeling like they were the "expert."

The assumption was that professionals who completed these trainings knew everything about the groups whose checklists they had completed, giving them tacit permission to take a place of power and control over their patients (or clients, or patrons). Tervalon and Murray-García challenged the notion of "culture as checklist" and argued in order to be truly effective in learning across difference, professionals (and the institutions to which they belong) must participate in a continuous process of learning called cultural humility. They named three key elements of the practice of cultural humility: lifelong learning and critical self-reflection, challenging power imbalances, and institutional accountability.

Lifelong Learning and Critical Self-Reflection

The concept of cultural humility embraces the importance of diversity training while cautioning that a single session can never be enough. One workshop, or even one college course, can't possibly cover all the elements or aspects of a racial, cultural, or socioeconomic group, let alone the many gradients and intersections it contains. For example, there are many important cultural differences between people who are labeled "Asian American," spanning native-born Americans as well as immigrants from Japan, Korea, China, the Philippines, India, Pakistan, and more. Even within one of those groups, there are differences that may not translate from one person's experience to another. People's history, family, community, education, and experiences have all shaped who they are, and those things change over time and from person to person. This is why Tervalon and Murray-García assert we must engage in learning throughout our lives, not in one-shot increments. We must be open to integrating new information as it comes to us. They also argue the most important teachers of culture are not educators with PhDs or consultants, but rather each individual who shares their unique story. They advocate for professionals to adopt a position of humility and respect of the expertise their patients or patrons have accumulated through their lived experiences. They—and we—recognize it can be difficult to be in the position of not knowing. It can feel much more comfortable to retreat into the armor of authority, but that can also prevent true connection and learning.

Karen fosters continuous learning among her staff through her weekly meetings. Each one occupies only a small amount of time, but together they form consistent encouragement for staff to question, assess, and learn from their experiences. This is also a form of reflective supervision, which creates a safe space for critical self-reflection—the counterpart to lifelong learning. The only way to see other people clearly is to see ourselves clearly first. Each practitioner—nurse, librarian, or social worker—must be willing to consider their own biases, their own preferences, and their own experiences, then be willing to confront how those things have shaped their ideas, values, beliefs, and ability to work with people who are culturally different. The blank PIE chart in appendix A can be one tool to begin to map this for yourself. Challenging yourself to examine these things is hard work and requires a lot of time and patience but can be facilitated by reflective practice, which we examine later in the chapter.

Challenge Power Imbalances

In chapter 5, we talked about the many ways librarians and even social workers can feel disempowered as advocates. This can make speaking up to challenge power imbalances especially difficult, but calling out those imbalances in order to make them visible is an important part of the process of cultural humility. As one library social worker told us, "If your social worker doesn't challenge you, you hired the wrong social worker." In this, as in all other collaborative work, the hard tasks should be shared by everyone involved. The section in chapter 4 on library social worker roles and communication touches on some of the strain social workers feel when they're expected to do most of the library's emotionally draining work, and expecting the social worker to be the first to challenge for change can be part of that strain if it's not shared mindfully among other staff. Similarly, libraries without social workers but wanting to implement or improve their social service connections will need to be prepared to take on awareness and the willingness to challenge inequities.

We can start by examining our profession as a whole in the same way we ask each person to examine themselves in critical self-reflection. As we noted in the introduction, social work and librarianship are not only female-dominated professions but also traditionally considered "feminine" jobs. This construction positions us to be and act in supporting roles in society. Besides being primarily female, both professions are majority white. Couple our inherent whiteness with the fact that the demographic served by both professions looks very different from the professionals doing the work, and it becomes clear that within our communities, we often have more collective power than our patrons. Of course, just as we don't want to make assumptions about our patrons based on generalizations about the type of background they may come from, each individual librarian or social worker will have a different relationship with their community. A white female who grew up in poverty but now works at an Ivy League college library, for example, will have a very different place within structures of power than an African American librarian who works in the community where he grew up. Both of their individual situations are entirely valid and worth understanding as a starting point from which they can speak up in their respective communities, as well as how much they might reasonably expect to accomplish. Their realities exist alongside and do not negate the fact that, taken as a whole, librarianship and social work are dominated by white females and therefore have a collective responsibility to use their privilege in service of empowering others.

The good news is the word "challenge" doesn't have to mean being aggressive or confrontational. Ursula's story in chapter 5 of creating a traveling art exhibit to share the stories of people experiencing homelessness, for example, shows one way to challenge power imbalances through education. One other example from Hennepin County Library is TransFabulous, a series of workshops bringing transgender youth together around creative pursuits (Griffith et al. 2018). The list of such programs is endless, and library staff reading this will likely already be thinking of their own examples. In the same way the library's existing relationships can be contextualized and shaped into a relationship-based reference collection, existing programs and activities can be gathered and placed within a framework of what the library does to promote equity in its community. Once you know what you're already doing, you can see what's missing and build momentum for further growth.

Institutional Accountability

In the workplace, cultural humility is also collective humility. It thrives where colleagues support each other and receive consistent reinforcement to persist in this difficult work. One of the greatest barriers to challenging power imbalances, though, can be the inability of people in power to hear and respond to those challenges. While many administrators and managers are open to change, there are others who may see any form of criticism or dissent as a personal attack. It can be easy for people who have power over others to forget this power is granted to them through our collective agreement to respect institutional hierarchy, rather than personal merit alone. That's why we see research in the news showing power can literally rewire the brain and make it more difficult to empathize with others (Useem 2017). Administrators and managers are key players in fostering cultural humility in their libraries, and they have a proportionately stronger mandate to be aware of their own privileges, how they relate to staff whose work lives they supervise or influence through decision making, and how their personal standing may influence policies and procedures impacting not only staff but entire communities.

We have emphasized throughout this book that administrative support for library-social work collaboration is key to lasting success, as reflected in the words of people we interviewed. Chue, who has been a front-line librarian for decades, would like to see administrators spend more time in public service so they don't just know but also viscerally experience the same challenges as their staff: "Some people are more involved in direct service, and [some are] less involved in direct service. It's a big challenge for managers and supervisors because they have so much stuff to do. They think that if they're wandering around in the library, seeing what is going on or talking to staff, that they have too many other things to do. I understand that feeling, but I just think it's pretty critical to do it." In addition to spending time on the ground, administrators who decide to hire library social workers should consider placing them in positions of hierarchical power, where they're able to influence decision making. Bradley said, "I would say being on the leadership and administration team as a manager has been very helpful on many levels as far as integrating social services models and tools into a totally different sector. Having all that support and leverage [helps me] influence policies and organization-wide training." Remember, policy development and educating others are key macro-level skills social workers can bring to the table.

Institutions are composed of people. While the person at the helm does have power—whether they're a rural library director who helps with everything from circulation to community relations, or a library dean whose days are composed of meetings and political maneuvers—staff members can also effect grassroots change. The best systems are ones where those efforts work in tandem, and one of the best ways to support work at all levels is reflective supervision.

Reflective Practice and Reflective Supervision

In social work, practitioners are required to engage in thousands of hours of "supervised" practice as a requirement for obtaining and maintaining their license. This doesn't mean social workers have a supervisor with them the entire time they are offering services. Rather, it means they meet with a more experienced social worker (often, but not always, their work supervisor) to process and review their experiences with clients. They discuss the decisions they made, the ethical dilemmas they faced, and the feelings their work brought forward. This process, known as reflective supervision, starts when social workers are in school, where they have to meet with a social work supervisor at least one hour each week as part of their field work (see chapter 3). Reflective supervision also gives practitioners an emotional outlet to learn how to deal with difficult and even traumatizing situations. Many of the encounters social work students and early social work practitioners face are new to them, and talking to someone with more experience helps them learn human service skills that are better conveyed through lived experience than through a textbook. This kind of supervision enables social workers to learn from their work and improve the services they provide.

Zelda, a library social worker, shared the kind of impact her work can have on her as an individual. This is the kind of emotional depletion reflective practice is meant to ameliorate:

> It can be really exhausting as a social worker to be the constant advocate for people who are stigmatized and are struggling around you all the time. That's something that is part of the [NASW] Code of Ethics, and that's something that we strive to do and are doing that constantly in our work with individuals and systematically. That includes our coworkers at the library and redirecting certain language and finding more strength-based vocabulary to help people to feel a bit better about the people that we are working with, to help decrease some of their vicarious trauma and stress. So it can be really exhausting to do that all day long every day.

Even though advocacy and great service are part of the core work of social workers and librarians, providing assistance to both patrons and staff takes its toll. Librarians who focus on public service also frequently face challenges that are new, unsettling, or outside the scope of their education, competence, or comfort. Taking time to reflect creates space to assess these situations to understand them better. Jakeem, a library administrator, decided to address this by "making sure that the staff has opportunities for self-care, or making sure that everyone has the opportunity to understand that they are probably going to hear some unpleasant things." Although the experiences Jakeem referred to were negative, he didn't shy away from exposing them, which is an important part of the process and responsibility of the supervisor.

So far, we've spoken of this approach as "reflective supervision," but a closely related term, and the one that may be most relevant for librarians, is "reflective practice." Social workers have structured their professional practice to include reflective supervision between the practitioner and another, more experienced, professional. However, there are other ways to get the benefit of reflection without this formal structure. Those options move beyond a supervisory dyad, so the broader term is "reflective practice." The questions we suggest you use to guide your reflection are based on the reflective learning model created by Graham Gibbs (1988). We've divided them into four broad phases.

1. **What happened?** Describe using facts. After that, explore feelings.
2. **What does it mean?** Evaluate: what was good or bad? Analyze: What did it mean?
3. **What are the takeaways?** What did you learn about yourself? What did you learn about others?
4. **What's next?** What will you do the same or differently in the future? What can change?

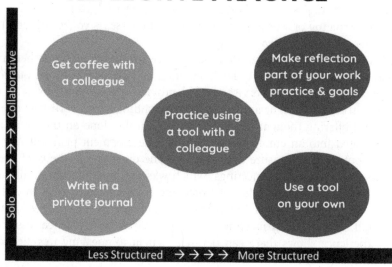

REFLECTIVE PRACTICE

Collaborative ↑ ↑ ↑ ↑ ↑ Solo

Get coffee with a colleague

Make reflection part of your work practice & goals

Practice using a tool with a colleague

Write in a private journal

Use a tool on your own

Less Structured → → → → More Structured

Figure 6.1

The thing to keep in in mind while answering these questions, whatever method you choose, is they're meant to externalize what happened. Whether it's on your own in a journal or at coffee with a coworker, you're working on pulling the experience outside of your mind and body so you can examine and release it. In our experience, this is often easier, especially for people who are new to this practice, if you have a structured tool at hand and work through it with someone else. For that reason, we include a worksheet in appendix F and the online resources that further breaks down these steps and provides more questions to prompt reflection.

In Figure 6.1, we map some suggestions for how reflective practice can be incorporated into library life. Keep in mind these options and the preceding questions work equally well with both negative and positive experiences. We often think first of reflective practice as a means of coping with challenges, but it's also a great way to learn from success and detail how to replicate it in the future.

If you prefer to reflect on your own, we suggest journaling or using the worksheet in appendix F. This allows you to record the details of what happens, your responses to it, and what you wish had gone better. By writing things out, you're intentionally slowing yourself down and reviewing the situation. You may discover new insights or perceive what happened in a different light. Another benefit to a written record is you can return to it in the future, either to remind yourself how you handled it or to document patron interactions to show a pattern of behavior or community needs over time. These could contribute to the kind of information we encourage collecting in other chapters to justify collaboration and hiring a social worker. The downside to journaling or working on your own, of course, is you're still getting only your own perspective.

Using the worksheet as a reflective practice tool along with another colleague carries the benefits of documentation as well as gaining an outside perspective. Ideally, a supervisor would provide time at work for staff to choose a trusted colleague and take turns responding to the worksheet questions and offering thoughtful feedback. This can be done on the fly or be incorporated into an employee's professional development plan, turning it into an outcome to measure over the year. The questions in the worksheet can also be used in staff meetings, which was the intention of one library branch manager when she left our preconference session at ALA in 2018. This is also similar to what Karen has been doing so successfully with her own staff, whose weekly meetings are, in effect, reflective practice sessions. Her experience shows there can be great benefit to engaging in reflection over time, even when it's done informally.

We mention going out for coffee with a colleague because even though this activity doesn't carry all the benefits of formal documentation, it's something many library staff already do. Whether it's coffee during a break or happy hour after work, these informal debriefing sessions can be just as valuable to long-term job satisfaction. We encourage managers and administrators to carve out space for reflection in the work day, but library staff as individuals still have power to reap the benefits of reflective practice by cultivating peer relationships.

Regardless of the method you choose for reflective practice or reflective supervision, know it's all part of a long-term process. Sometimes a reflection will yield great insights, but other times it might not. Reflection isn't meant to make everything better—it's a tool to make working life more understandable and tolerable by making small, but meaningful, adjustments that accumulate over time.

Online Resources

www.wholepersonlibrarianship.com/book/resources/chapter6

- Links to:
  - Cultural humility documentary with interviews with original authors
  - The Wakanheza Project
- Printable version of the reflective practice worksheet (see also appendix F)
- Additional resources provided by you and your colleagues

Conclusion

Future Directions

> *As a teacher of new, up-and-coming students often faced with this idea that libraries are disappearing, or they're changing because everything is going online, and everything is becoming digital, and we always try to teach them that, you know, it's more than about the books. It's about information and knowledge, and so I think it's just really important to realize there are no hard boundaries as to what we offer as librarians and libraries. That it's more an emphasis on sharing information and knowledge to help somebody.*
> —Isadora, PhD candidate in library and information science

Library-social work collaboration is growing exponentially. By the time this book is published, some of the information in it will already be out of date. Everyone has been so busy working that there has barely been time to pause, reflect, and share information. However, there are signs of an impending proliferation of opportunities for research, learning, and growth. We're excited to be able to touch on a few of them here and watch in the coming years for conference sessions and publications from our many new colleagues in this work.

Libraries as Social Work Host Sites

From the social work perspective, libraries represent a new area of education, practice, and scholarship. As we noted in chapter 3, the proliferation of libraries in the United States is a vast, untapped network of locations for student internships. As library-social work collaborations continue to grow and find secure funding, professional social workers also will have many more opportunities to specialize in this niche. Interest among social work students and faculty started slowly but is rapidly catching up to the pace of interest from libraries. At the CSWE Annual Program Meeting in 2018, we gave a presentation that was one of four focused on library-social work collaboration, each led by a different set of academics speaking to dozens of interested participants. Many people in the audience had been participating in similar collaborations, internships, education, and writing about social work pilot projects in libraries, without realizing until that moment they had so much company. They shared contact information and came together in discussions about evaluation methods, curriculum design, sample learning contracts, funding sources, future presentations, and how to continue networking. One of the resources we shared widely was the new website, Social Work Students & Public Libraries (www.mswstudentsinlibraries.com), run by Sarah Johnson, a reference and instruction librarian and assistant professor at Hunter College in New York City. Sarah has master's degrees in both library science and social work and has worked in both fields, so she's well positioned to lead research, collaboration, and mentorship in this niche of the field.

Unlike librarians, social workers are accustomed to working at locations that aren't primarily focused on them and their work. They have a professional term for this: the "host site." Typically, these sites would be hospitals, clinics, schools, nonprofit agencies, and the many other organizations that employ social workers. This means they already have a place in their conceptual structure to slot the library's role. Meanwhile, librarians have been struggling to incorporate the new library social worker position into a massive shift in roles and responsibilities. The transition in librarianship calls for a response as extensive as this book, but the transition in social work will likely be much smoother.

Social Work Education for Library School Students

This book focuses on practice, and we asked about and have made recommendations for education of professionals in the field. Nevertheless, we heard from several people they'd like to see changes to library school education to reflect these changes in the field. Devon, who directs a small suburban library system, said, "I would love to see in terms of the profession at least the exploration of the idea of library science and social work as a combined or dual degree program. . . . I bring this up because I was invited to participate in a panel discussion for our local graduate school of library and information science, who were doing a retreat to look at potential revision to their curricula. One of the things I mentioned was to consider developing either a track within the library school program or potentially reaching out to the school of social work and exploring the possibility of some type of dual-degree program." We do know of one dual-degree program that has existed quietly for a number of years at Dominican University in Chicago, Illinois, but we also know from our own conversations with schools that establishing crossover courses can present significant logistical challenges. This has partly to do with the nature of academia and partly with the fact that social work degree requirements are more tightly structured than those in library science, leaving less wiggle room to incorporate electives.

Alongside the development of dual-degree programs, there is also plenty of space for library schools to adjust their approach to incorporate relevant social work methods. Isadora, a PhD candidate in library and information science at the time she spoke to us, brought a valuable perspective to this conversation. She said,

> A lot of our students are going to end up working in public libraries and dealing with all sorts of different issues, [like] drugs, homelessness. . . . I can see how we don't have the resources to teach a class like that, but I don't even remember it being mentioned that you're going to have to meet certain patron issues. I don't know how to address it because obviously we're not social workers, we are not training people to do that, but it should at least be acknowledged that there will be things that you will come up against.

Alecia concurred, saying, "In my library specifically, librarians said that their program didn't ever really talk about advocacy or social justice. So coming back to where libraries and social workers can collaborate, I think that maybe the library programs need to change a little bit too."

We recognize making changes to degree options within a complicated accreditation structure can be daunting. Sara helped work on a piece of her library school's accreditation report when she was a student and participated in interviews for their recent reaccreditation, so she had a small taste of the smorgasbord of documentation required. Mary, of course, is now a professor and intimately familiar with the educational standards for social work accreditation. But from a library education perspective, this circles all the way back to where Sara began six years ago, as a library school student in need of the training and resources social workers can provide. As library schools, and their PhD programs in particular, continue to consolidate around an information science approach at the expense of human services, collaborations with schools of social work can offer a much-needed counterbalance.

Multiple Social Workers in a Library System

While many library systems have followed the San Francisco model of one social worker supervising multiple outreach workers, the addition of multiple social workers within the same system is still very new. Denver Public Library had four social workers as of June 2018: three are supervised by the original hire there, Elissa Hardy, in addition to their outreach workers, known as peer navigators (GSSW 2018). Mary Olive Joyce, featured as a supervisor at Kansas City Public Library (KCPL) in chapter 3, has been able to use both her library background and social work degree to grow KCPL's outreach department from 4 employees to 14. That total includes AmeriCorps volunteers and graduate-level social work interns, one staff member dedicated to refugee and immigrant services, and Jason's full-time position overseeing community resources and vulnerable populations. There are likely many more examples in the works.

One of the questions raised in chapter 4, which continues to be an issue for many library social workers, is position sustainability. Systems that have found the resources to transition from a single worker to whole departments may provide some models for sustainability going forward. They also raise the specter of social workers replacing librarians, something we believe is unlikely but has been expressed as both a recommendation and a fear from library staff. Libraries continue to define a post-internet role that incorporates multiple collaborations, from digital humanities in academia to cultural liaisons at public libraries. Social workers are one more partner in this human web of improved patron services.

Whole Person Library Management

Another area where we've seen intense interest in social work methodology is library management. Isadora suggested, "Maybe it would be an option to have in library science education, for people who are really interested in library management, to at least have a session on [social work concepts] instead of just putting it in a regular library curriculum." She made the suggestion in part from a logistical mindset of where to begin curriculum integration, but this reflects a larger need. At our training sessions, library managers both with and without library degrees have been interested in engaging their employees in reflective supervision, applying cultural humility to shape their workplace environments, and using PIE to empathize with staff concerns. This is a natural extension of incorporating a social work model into patron services: staff members should be accorded the same level of understanding and respect that libraries offer to their patrons. Not only does this cultivate the mental and emotional health staff members need in order to generate empathy for patrons, but it also gives tools to managers who are at least as hungry as the public service workers they supervise for guidance on providing human (and humane) service. Popular management models grounded in for-profit business can only address part of the experience of working in an environment where staff are personally motivated to help other people and where money-making is barely a concern. We expect to delve into this as a next step to explore in our library research and training.

Professional Involvement and Professional Organizations

In chapter 4, we touched on how important it is for library social workers to connect with each other, but the scope of this book demonstrates interest and involvement stretch across many boundaries in our fields. Library staff and social workers who are engaged in all aspects of this work—from the front lines to students to researchers and beyond—are looking for the best ways to connect as professionals. As library social worker Yusef said, "My biggest recommendation would be to connect with other libraries. . . . We just started doing it because there is a community need, and the library reached out to our street outreach teams to get some help, but just hearing what different people are doing and really looking into other libraries would be the starting point." Libraries looking into creating new programs have been very proactive about reaching out to existing library social workers, and those social workers help when they can, but we've also had a lot of conversation about how to create a central space for everyone to connect so the burden doesn't always fall on the same highly visible few.

Finding a single professional home for everyone presents a challenge given we have separate professional organizations as librarians and social workers. On top of that, many people in both professions who are interested in this kind of collaboration may not be members, or if they are members of one wouldn't want to spend more money on another organizational membership. Some of the options under consideration or development, along with their pros and cons, include:

- **Public Library Association (PLA):** The core group of library social workers who authored a recent letter to *American Libraries* magazine outlining their agenda for libraries (Jeske et al. 2018) have been increasingly involved with PLA, forming a Social Work Task Force to begin to organize themselves as public library leaders. However, PLA is one division within ALA and doesn't encompass the growing number of academic librarians who are interested in these collaborations or the state library systems that fund many new library-social work collaborations.

- **Council of Social Work Education (CSWE):** As mentioned earlier, faculty members of CSWE are excited to come together around their role in placing and mentoring students in libraries. Their 2018 conference was the first to include multiple peer-reviewed sessions on the topic. But this is also a fairly exclusive group, with a focus on academics more than practitioners in the field.

- **National Association of Social Work (NASW) and Its State Chapters:** Justine Janis, a library social worker in Illinois, has made some progress establishing a shared interest group within her NASW state chapter (Janis

2018), which could be a useful option for local conversation in other states as well. NASW is aware of these efforts, but has not yet established a formal group at the national level.

- **Association of Bookmobile and Outreach Services (ABOS):** One participant in our interviews suggested growing a division within ABOS, which has a relevant focus and low membership dues. This could be an option that would cut across silos in librarianship, although awareness and reach of the association may be lower than it is for larger organizations.

- **American Library Association Membership Initiative Groups (ALA MIG):** Sara considered applying for status as a MIG, which is granted for three years as a way to bring like-minded professionals together at ALA conferences. It would provide official meeting space on the conference agenda without forcing membership in a specific division or round table. However, MIGs are meant to be temporary and eventually disband or be absorbed into a sponsoring unit.

Some or all of these options may grow into full-fledged organizational efforts, but none on its own presents a comprehensive solution to bring together everyone who has an interest in this work. We will continue to support, encourage, and share news about these efforts through the WPL website, which provides a low-barrier point of entry for anyone to become part of the library-social work community, regardless of professional, educational, or national silos. Our blog has an open form to use to contribute posts with news about new work, the e-mail list is a place for questions and connections, and we encourage additions to the calendar of events. We feel it's especially important in this time of rapid growth that all of us come together to share our views and help each other navigate this evolving landscape.

Online Resources

www.wholepersonlibrarianship.com/book/resources/future

- Links to:
  - Association options for collaborative membership
  - Dominican University's joint MLIS-MSW program
- Additional resources provided by you and your colleagues

PIE Chart Worksheet

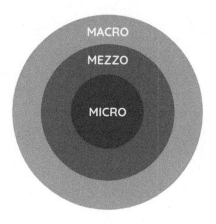

Individual or Group for PIE:			
	Micro Level	Mezzo Level	Macro Level
What are some possible **influences** on this individual or group?			
What are some **interventions** the library can offer in response to these influences?			

Community Needs Assessment

To begin a community needs assessment, it is important to first define the community you want to assess. This is typically going to be spatially defined, along the boundaries of the library's service area, but there may be groups within or outside of the geographic location that may need to be considered. For example, your library might want to start a program like the one highlighted in chapter 1 and would want to focus on the needs of the Somali community within a particular neighborhood.

Collecting this information may require holding key informant interviews or focus groups, and you will need to connect and network with other groups and organizations within your community to gather the required information.

The goal of a needs assessment is to help you better understand the community and the role the library can play in best serving the needs of its patrons. Therefore, feel free to add, delete, or change any part of this tool in order to make it work best for your library and community.

Community Overview

Find or create a map showing the boundaries of the area you are assessing. Explain why you chose these boundaries.

Walk and drive through the community along the boundaries you have determined. What can you observe about the community? What do you notice about the people, the houses, the structures, the roads, the commerce, and the recreational facilities?

Population Characteristics

- What is the size of the community?
- What is the age and gender distribution of the community?

- What nationality and ethnicity comprises the community (if appropriate, address the role more recent immigrants have played in the community—e.g., Somali in Minneapolis/St. Paul, Hmong and Karen in St. Paul)?
- What is the impact of the population characteristics on neighborhood/community?

Income

- What is the annual income of the community?
- What is the annual income of subgroups within the community (e.g. women, people of color, veterans)?
- What is the poverty rate of the community?
- What is the impact of income on the neighborhood/community?

Community Attractiveness

- What characteristics attract and hold residents, such as climate, geography, cost of living? What characteristics detract from the attractiveness of the community?
- What is the impact of community attractiveness on the neighborhood/community?

Cultural/Civic Systems

- Are there parks? What kind of condition are they in? Who uses them? Where are they located?
- Are there community centers in the community? Whom do they serve?
- Are there other libraries in the community? How far away?
- What other cultural resources are available within the community? How accessible are they?
- What recreational activities does the community hold? How accessible are they? Who uses them?
- Are there social clubs? How inclusive or exclusive are they?
- What civic organizations exist? Who belongs or doesn't belong?
- What role does volunteering and civic engagement play in the community? Who participates and doesn't participate in volunteering or civic engagement?
- What is the impact of cultural/civic systems on the neighborhood/community?

Housing

- What kind of housing is available in the community (rental properties, owned properties, apartments, houses, duplexes)?
- What condition is the housing in?
- What is the average cost of housing in the community? How affordable is housing given the economic conditions of the community?
- Is there a population of people experiencing homelessness in the community? Who are they? Where do they find shelter or respite?
- What is the impact of housing on the neighborhood/community?

Commerce and Industry

- Who are the major employers and industries in the community?
- What is the unemployment rate of the community? What is the unemployment rate of subgroups within the community (younger people, people of color, women, men, older adults)?
- What is the future development potential of the community?
- How stable are businesses in the community?
- Are there accessible grocery stores in the community?
- Is there a strong union presence in the community?
- What is the impact of commerce and industry on the neighborhood/community?

Transportation

- What is the main mode of transportation in the community?
- How expensive is gas in the community?
- Is there public transportation available in the community?
- How affordable and accessible is public transportation in the community?
- What condition are the roads in the community?
- Are there sidewalks or bike paths in the community?
- What options are there for people who have challenges in travelling (e.g., the elderly, people with disabilities, parents with small children, adolescents who can't drive)?
- What is the impact of transportation on the community?

Law Enforcement

- Is there a police presence in the community?
- How is law enforcement regarded in the community?
- How diverse (ethnically, age, gender) is the police force serving the community?
- Are there any jails, prisons, or juvenile detention centers in the community?
- What is the impact of law enforcement on the community?

Education

- Are there schools in the community? What kind (elementary, middle, high, technical or community, universities, colleges)?
- What conditions are the schools in?
- What is the education level of the community?
- What is the education level of subgroups within the community?
- Is there community education, parent education, or early childhood education (preschool) in the community?
- Are there childcare centers or home childcare options within the community?
- Who uses the educational resources in the community?
- What impact does education have on the community?

Governmental Types

- Is there a city manager, mayor, or city council?
- Describe the decision makers in the community: Who are they? How long have they served? How well do they represent the community?
- How involved is the community in the decision-making process?
- What is the impact of government on the community?

Religion and Churches

- How many places of worship are there? What denomination is most prevalent? What impact does this have on the community?
- What role does religion/churches play in the community?

Health

- How healthy is the community (e.g., rates of heart disease, stroke, asthma, smoking, cancer, alcoholism, substance use)?

- How active is the community?
- Are there fresh fruits and vegetables available in the community? How accessible are they?
- What health systems (e.g., hospitals, medical clinics, nursing homes, dental hospitals, mental health clinics, chiropractic and naturopathic centers) are available to the community?
- Whom do the health systems serve?
- How accessible are the social/health systems in the community?
- What problems and limitations do the social and health systems have?
- What is the impact of health on the community?

Social Services

- What and where are the primary social service (public, private: for-profit and nonprofit) agencies (e.g., county social services, child protection shelters, homeless shelters, domestic violence shelters, immigrant and refugee services, economic assistance offices, employment services, sexual assault and trafficking services, alcohol or substance use services)?
- Whom do the social services serve?
- How accessible are the social services in the community?
- What problems and limitations do the social services have?
- What informal helping systems exist within the community?
- What is the impact of social services on the neighborhood/community?

Environment

- Are there any major environmental hazards within the community? Where are these located? Whom do they most affect?
- How is the air quality of the community?
- How is the water quality of the community?
- How is waste disposed of? Where is it disposed?
- Is there recycling in this community? How easy is it to recycle?
- Is lead or asbestos a concern in this community?
- What is the impact of the environment on the community?

Conclusion

- Based on your walk-through/drive-through, and the information you collected from various data sources, what are your overall impressions of the community?

- What are the strengths of this community?
- What are the needs of the community?
- What role can the library play in meeting the identified needs of the community?
- How would you go about assessing the viability of any intervention or programming the library would create?
- How would you go about implementing your identified solutions?
- How would you evaluate your interventions for success?

Learning Contract Template

Name of University:
Dates of Contract:

Names and Contact Information

- Student
- Field Instructor
- Faculty Field Liaison
- Task Supervisor
- Agency (Host Site)

Structure

Most social work internship learning contracts will include the following information:

- CSWE Competencies
- Learning Activities
- Learning Outcomes
- Dates or Timeline for Completion
- Status/Comments to assist with evaluation and progress

Purpose

The field instructor and the student usually complete the learning contract within the first few weeks of the internship. The purpose of developing the learning contract is to prompt conversation between students and their field instructor regarding the potential learning opportunities available through the internship. Often, a signed hard copy is required for the social work faculty field instructor.

Evaluation

The learning contract is typically used to evaluate progress of social work students midway through their placement and again at the end of the internship.

Many programs use a scale to evaluate progress and achievement of the stated learning outcomes. For example:

Evaluation Scale		
1	Not met*	Does not meet professional expectations
2	Limited	Demonstrates limited understanding of the skills/practice behaviors and shows some ability to implement into practice. Is not fully proficient
3	Competent	Demonstrates a sufficient understanding of the skills/practice behaviors and is able to implement and integrate them into practice most of the time. Meets expectations
4	Excels**	Demonstrates consistent and effective implementation and integration of skills/practice behaviors in practice; exceeds professional expectations.

* Use if students have not had an opportunity to practice yet

** Only to be used in the final semester

Learning Contract

Most programs require students to identify one or more outcomes for each of the 10 CSWE Competencies. Sample learning outcomes are detailed in the table on the next page.

The remaining competencies would each have their own table for ratings, deadlines, and comments, in the same format. For the sake of space here, example outcomes and tasks are listed for the remaining competencies outside of the separate evaluation table format.

Competency 2: Engage Diversity and Difference in Practice

Learning Outcomes for Competency 2:

- Research and apply knowledge of the specific populations using the library to enhance the well-being of patrons in a manner that recognizes the importance of culture and ethnicity in all stages of social work interventions.

Competency 1: Demonstrate ethical and professional behavior		
Learning Outcomes for Competency 1	Mid-Placement Evaluation	Final Evaluation
Develop, manage, and maintain at least five ongoing relationships with homeless patrons using the library. Understand and apply the core values of social work and its unique perspective in relation to working effectively with library staff in an interdisciplinary team.		
Employ strategies of ethical reasoning in a library setting, paying attention to policy and value conflicts between social work and library service delivery, personal values and biases, and social work ethics.		
Overall Rating		
Comments:		

Learning Activities/Tasks *This is where the student will list out the tasks or activities they plan to complete in order to achieve the learning outcomes listed earlier.*	Completion Dates
Complete reflective journal for processing during supervision.	Monthly
Bring social work perspective to multidisciplinary interactions within the agency and community.	Throughout
Complete agency orientation and shadow supervisor for two weeks.	By end of week 2
When introducing self to new patrons, identify myself as a social worker and progressively take a leadership stance, with a collaborative emphasis, when making referrals.	Throughout
Expand identification as social worker by engaging in more advanced practice, direct service role throughout the semester when engaging patrons.	By end of week 8
Consult NASW Code of Ethics and ALA Code of Ethics: Identify/ manage conflicting priorities between the two and discuss during supervision.	By end of week 2
Ethics Paper: Reflect on ethical dilemmas in field within required ethical dilemma paper.	By end of week 9
Comments:	

Competency 3: Advance Human Rights and Social, Economic, and Environmental Justice

Learning Outcomes for Competency 3:

- Use knowledge of the oppression, discrimination, and historical trauma on library patrons and their support networks to promote self-sufficiency, self-advocacy, and empowerment.

Competency 4: Engage in Research-Informed Practice and Practice-Informed Research

Learning Outcomes for Competency 4:

- Apply knowledge from literature, and evidence-informed practice in work with library patrons and community partners.

Competency 5: Engage in Policy Practice

Learning Outcomes for Competency 5:

- Manage individual (personal) and multi-stakeholder (interpersonal) processes at the local, national, and international levels to inspire and leverage power and resources to optimize services and outcomes.

Competencies 6–9: Engage (6), Assess (7), Intervene (8), and Evaluate (9) with Individuals, Families, Groups, Organizations, and Communities

Learning Outcomes for Competencies 6–9:

- Establish a culturally responsive therapeutic relationship that encourages service participants to be equal partners in the establishment of goals for intervention and referrals (6).
- Systematically gather information from multiple sources to assess service participants' coping strategies to reinforce and improve adaptation to life situations, circumstances, and events (7).
- Critically evaluate, select, and apply best practices and evidence-informed interventions with patrons needing social work services (8).
- Evaluate the process and outcomes to develop best practice interventions for a range of bio-psycho-social-spiritual conditions with patrons needing social work services (9).

Learning Activities/Tasks	Aligned to Outcome #	Completion Dates
Attend cultural competency staff training.	2	By end of week 4
Work with Refugee and Immigrant Services Outreach Team to meet and provide services to immigrant and refugee patrons.	2	Throughout
Engage in collaborative partnerships with at least six local agencies representing diverse populations to provide services for our underserved populations within the library.	2	By end of week 10
Present information on library resources to participants of offender re-entry program and conduct focus group based on the participants' needs.	2	By end of week 8
Advocate for the rights of marginalized within the library by ensuring access to resources and materials by conducting needs assessments of all branches.	3	By end of internship
Leverage resources to empower the oppressed by creating programs directly serving their needs.	3	By midterm
Engage with library patrons through "Coffee & Conversation" program.	3	By end of week 5
Complete voter registration training and advocate for homeless individual's right to vote "You Don't Need a Home to Vote" campaign.	3	By end of week 10
Begin attending meeting for annual "Point in Time" count of individuals experiencing homelessness.	3	Weeks 5–12
Take part in Youth Committee in preparation for capturing an accurate youth count for the annual point in time event.	3	Weeks 7–12
Discuss and develop research question for research project on serving the homeless.	4	By midterm
Compile literature reviews on social work/social services programs in public libraries.	4	By week 10

(continued)

Research promising library/social work collaborations for possible replication at the library.	4	By week 2
Develop questions for focus group, based on research.	4	By week 5
Conduct focus group.	4	By week 8
Work to formulate organizational (library) policies that improve the well-being of underserved library patrons.	5	By end of semester
Based on evaluation of library policies, reformulate and propose a more current/ updated policy (re: general expectations of customer behavior or Sunshine Law as it relates to incident reports—as potential topics. What research exists? What are other libraries doing?).	5	By end of week 11
Complete voter registrar training.	5	By end of week 4
Meet with library branch manager and reference manager to discuss ethical dilemmas and fair enforcement regarding library patron code of conduct to improve library policies.	5	By midterm
Research best practices of other urban libraries regarding code of conduct and policies that might unfairly target those experiencing poverty and/or homelessness.	5	By end of placement
Research policies around engagement with older adults.	5	By end of week 15
Research library policies and engage in policy practice regarding access to services for older adults.	5	By end of placement
Utilize monthly "Coffee & Conversation" events to engage with underserved patrons in order to get a sense of who they are and to deliver effective, relevant programming.	6	By end of week 5
Patron Strengths/Needs Assessment: conduct during outreach events, "Coffee & Conversation."	7	By end of week 5

Work with patrons experiencing homelessness to tutor them on photo taking and to curate their photo selection in preparation for art show.	8	By end of placement
Analyze surveys given to patrons and evaluate/implement library programming based on data.	9	By end of week 12

Mid-Placement Evaluation: Overall, this student has performed at the following level in field instruction:

- Not competent
- Limited competency
- Competent
- Excel

Additional Comments and Feedback:

Signatures from:

- Student
- Field Instructor
- Task Supervisor
- Faculty Liaison

Final Evaluation: Overall, this student has performed at the following level in field instruction:

- Not competent
- Limited competency
- Competent
- Excel

Additional Comments and Feedback:

Signatures from:

- Student
- Field Instructor
- Task Supervisor
- Faculty Liaison

Sample Intake Form

Date:	Do you have a library card? Yes No
Name:	Date of Birth:
City and Zip:	Employed? Yes No
Gender:	Race/Ethnicity:

Who lives with you in your home? You don't have to list yourself.

1. Name:	Date of Birth:	Relation:
2. Name:	Date of Birth:	Relation:
3. Name:	Date of Birth:	Relation:

What would you like assistance with today? There is no charge for this service.

Education
- ☐ FAFSA
- ☐ Literacy
- ☐ Education

Financial Assistance
- ☐ Family Independence (TANF)
- ☐ Income Taxes
- ☐ Social Security Insurance/Disability

Health
- ☐ Health Insurance
- ☐ Vision/Dental Needs
- ☐ Prescription Assistance
- ☐ Health Concerns
- ☐ Hygiene Kit

Individual and Family
- ☐ Parenting or Family Concerns
- ☐ Veterans Benefits

(continued)

☐ Employment

☐ Financial Planning

Food

☐ SNAP Application (Food Stamps)

☐ Food Pantry Referrals

Housing

☐ Housing Referral Assistance

☐ Shelter/Temporary Housing

☐ Property Tax Exemption

☐ Legal Assistance

☐ Clothing and Furniture

Other

☐ Library Card

☐ Voter Registration

☐ Counseling

☐ Other (specify):

If you agree to be contacted, please leave your contact information. Richland Library will not share this information with anyone without your express permission.	
By mail at:	
By phone at:	*(xxx) xxx-xxxx—We cannot text*
By e-mail at:	

Sample Staff Survey

The contents of this survey are a modification of the form used by Richland Library in Columbia, South Carolina. On the reverse of this form, the library includes all of its legal disclosures in plain language.

Social Worker Program at Central
For the last two years, the Free Library has hosted social workers at Parkway Central, in partnership with the Department of Behavioral Health and disAbility Services. The service was launched to help patrons in need of social services, to alleviate difficult situations, and to offer support for staff. Though anecdotal responses have been positive, we now would like to document your reaction in order to consider potential for growth. Please take a few minutes to answer this anonymous survey. Your opinions are very important.
What is your job title?
How long have you worked at Central?   ☐ 1–2 years   ☐ 2–4 years   ☐ 4+ years
Do you know that there are social workers available in the library to help patrons in need?   ☐ Yes   ☐ No
Do you know how to contact the social workers if you or a patron needs assistance?   ☐ Yes   ☐ No

(continued)

Have you interacted directly with the social workers?

☐ Yes

☐ No

If "no," why not?

If "yes," how often?

☐ Weekly

☐ Monthly

☐ Occasionally

☐ Once or twice

If "yes," which of the following were the issues being addressed? (check any that apply)

☐ Patron in need of social services

☐ Patron disturbing to library staff and/or other patrons

☐ Emergency

☐ Personal reasons

☐ Other

If "Other" please describe:

Was there a resolution to the issue?

☐ Yes

☐ No

How do you feel when you encounter patrons who are in need of social services? (check any that apply)

Unsafe				Safe
1	2	3	4	5

Unconfident				Confident
1	2	3	4	5

Helpless				Capable
1	2	3	4	5

Stressed				Relaxed
1	2	3	4	5

Unhappy				Happy
1	2	3	4	5

Uncomfortable				Comfortable
1	2	3	4	5

Have these feelings or your attitude changed since the start of the social worker program? Please explain.

If you have interacted with the social workers and have a story about how the situation was resolved, please share it here.

Is there anything else you'd like to share about your experience with the social worker program?

Do you have any ideas for additional programs or services like this one?

This form was created by the Free Library of Philadelphia as part of their participation in the Building Evaluation Capacity Initiative.

Reflective Practice Worksheet

Reflective Practice Worksheet

Think about something that happened, good or bad, that you want to understand better. Follow the prompts on your own first and then share with a partner for feedback and clarification.

Stage	Questions Adapted from Gibbs 1988	Response Notes
What happened?	**Description:** What happened? Don't make judgments yet; simply describe.	
	Feelings: How did you feel during the event? How did you feel after? Again, just describe.	
What did it mean?	**Evaluation:** What was good or bad about the experience? Now is the time to make value judgments.	
	Analysis: What sense can you make of the situation? What do you think was really going on? Bring in ideas and opinions from outside the experience to help you.	

(continued)

What are the takeaways?	**Personal conclusions:** What can you conclude from this analysis about the ways you as an individual work and think?	
	General conclusions: What other conclusions can you make about this type of interaction in general?	
What's next?	**Action plan:** What are you going to do the same or differently in this type of situation next time? What steps can you take now, based on what you've learned?	

References

ALA. 2015. "One Year Later: An Interview with Ferguson (Mo.) Library Director Scott Bonner." Tools, Publications & Resources. August 6. http://www.ala.org/tools/librariestransform/libraries-transforming-communities/blog/one-year-later-interview-ferguson-mo-library-director-scott.

ALA. 2017. "Professional Ethics." Tools, Publications & Resources. May 19. http://www.ala.org/tools/ethics.

Back, John David. 2018. "Are There More Libraries or McDonald's?—John David Back—Medium." *Medium*. May 7. https://medium.com/@johndavidback/are-there-more-libraries-or-mcdonalds-26ca5b069a4.

Bausman, Margaret. 2016. "A Case Study of the Progressive Era Librarian Edith Guerrier: The Public Library, Social Reform, 'New Women', and Urban Immigrant Girls." *Library & Information History* 32 (4): 272–92. doi:10.1080/17583489.2016.1220782.

Box, Dennis. 2017. "King County Library System 2016 Highlights." *Covington-Maple Valley Reporter*. January 30. http://www.maplevalleyreporter.com/news/king-county-library-system-2016-highlights/.

CBC News. 2013. "Winnipeg Library's In-House Social Worker Offers Help." CBC. December 13. https://www.cbc.ca/news/canada/manitoba/winnipeg-library-s-in-house-social-worker-offers-help-1.2462471.

Council on Social Work Education. 2015. "Educational Policy and Accreditation Standards for Baccalaureate and Master's Social Work Programs." Council on Social Work Education. https://www.cswe.org/getattachment/Accreditation/Standards-and-Policies/2015-EPAS/2015EPASandGlossary.pdf.aspx.

Council on Social Work Education. 2018. "2017 Statistics on Social Work Education in the United States." https://www.cswe.org/Research-Statistics/Research-Briefs-and-Publications/CSWE_2017_annual_survey_report-FINAL.aspx.

Dallas Library. 2014. "What Is the Library Doing to Address the Issue of Homelessness?" Booked Solid. October 16. http://dallaslibrary2.org/blogs/

bookedSolid/2014/10/what-is-the-library-doing-to-address-the
-issue-of-homelessness/.

Estreicher, Deborah. 2013. "A Brief History of the Social Workers in the Library
Program." Whole Person Librarianship. May 5. https://wholepersonli
brarianship.com/2013/05/05/a-brief-history-of-the-social-workers-in-the
-library-program/.

Fernald, Anne, Virginia A. Marchman, and Adriana Weisleder. 2013. "SES Differences in Language Processing Skill and Vocabulary Are Evident at 18
Months." *Developmental Science* 16 (2): 234–48. doi:10.1111/desc.12019.

Ford, Anne. 2018a. "Bringing Harassment Out of the History Books: Addressing
the Troubling Aspects of Melvil Dewey's Legacy." *American Libraries*
49 (6): 48–52. https://americanlibrariesmagazine.org/2018/06/01/
melvil-dewey-bringing-harassment-out-of-the-history-books/.

Ford, Anne. 2018b. "2018 Annual Wrap-Up." *American Libraries*. July 18. https://
americanlibrariesmagazine.org/2018/07/18/2018-annual-wrap-up/.

Gibbs, Graham. 1988. "Learning by Doing: A Guide to Teaching and Learning
Methods." Oxford Brookes. https://thoughtsmostlyaboutlearning.files
.wordpress.com/2015/12/learning-by-doing-graham-gibbs.pdf.

Goodman, Amy, and David Goodman. 2008. "America's Most Dangerous Librarians." *Mother Jones.* September/October. https://www.motherjones.com/
politics/2008/09/americas-most-dangerous-librarians.

Griffith, Michelle, Dylan Miettinen, Jack Warrick, and Paul Hodowanic. 2018.
"TransFabulous Provides Creative Outlet—One Medium at a Time." *Minnesota Daily.* October 14. http://www.mndaily.com/article/2018/10/a
-transfabulous-provides-creative-outlet-one-medium-at-a-time.

GSSW. 2018. "Library Social Work." Graduate School of Social Work at Denver
University. June 26. https://socialwork.du.edu/news/library-social-work.

Hatch, Caslon. 2017. "Loussac Library Sees Uptick in Patrons, More Residents
Seeking Social Services." November 6. http://www.ktuu.com/content/
news/Loussac-Library-sees-uptick-in-patrons-more-residents-seeking
-social-work-services-455703973.html.

Henry, Meghan, Anna Mahathey, Tyler Morrill, Anna Robinson, Azim Shivji,
and Rian Watt. 2018. "The 2018 Annual Homeless Assessment Report
(AHAR) to Congress." December. https://www.hudexchange.info/
resources/documents/2018-AHAR-Part-1.pdf.

Hines, Samantha. 2015. "Connecting Individuals with Social Services: The
Library's Role." IFLA World Library and Information Congress. http://
www.ifla.org/files/assets/reference-and-information-services/
publications/512-hines-en.pdf.

"Home Is Where the Books Are." 2018. Hennepin County Library. April 20.
https://www.hclib.org/about/news/2018/April/upper-post.

IFSW. 2018. "Global Social Work Statement of Ethical Principles." International
Federation of Social Workers. July 2. https://www.ifsw.org/global-social
-work-statement-of-ethical-principles/.

Janis, Justine. 2018. "Public Library Social Work: An Emerging Field." National Association of Social Work Illinois Chapter. June 11. http://naswil.org/news/chapter-news/featured/public-library-social-work-an-emerging-field/.

Jeske, Michelle, Elissa Hardy, Tom Fortin, Leah Esguerra, Nick Higgins, Ashley Horn, Oliver Sanidas, Linda Speas, Brendan Haggerty, Mary Olive Joyce, Jason Pearl, and Peter Bromberg. 2018. "Letter from Public Library Directors and Social Workers | American Libraries Magazine." *American Libraries.* September 4. https://americanlibrariesmagazine.org/blogs/the-scoop/letter-from-public-library-directors-and-social-workers/.

Krier, Laura. 2012. "Hunger, Homelessness, and Poverty Task Force (HHPTF)." Round Tables. April 26. http://www.ala.org/rt/srrt/hunger-homelessness-and-poverty-task-force-hhptf.

Miller, Rebecca T. 2018. "Farewell to Fines." *Library Journal* 143 (12): 8.

NASW. 2018. "Code of Ethics." National Association of Social Workers. https://www.socialworkers.org/About/Ethics/Code-of-Ethics/Code-of-Ethics-English.

"National Social Work Month." 2015. Free Library of Philadelphia. March 14. https://libwww.freelibrary.org/blog/post/2206.

NCES. 2018. "2015–16 National Postsecondary Student Aid Study (NPSAS:16)." National Center for Education Statistics. May 15. https://nces.ed.gov/surveys/npsas/.

"New Community Resource Specialist—The Seattle Public Library Foundation." 2018. Accessed August 5. http://foundation.spl.org/2016/11/new-community-resource-specialist/.

Nienow, Mary. 2017. "The Professional Socialization of Macro Practice Social Workers: A Narrative Inquiry." http://hdl.handle.net/11299/195383.

"Pilot Program Will Connect Library Patrons to State Services." 2018. State of Delaware News. January 2. https://news.delaware.gov/2018/01/02/social-workers-libraries/.

"Selection of Resolutions Adopted by the ALA Council." 2018. About ALA. Accessed September 30. http://www.ala.org/aboutala/selection-resolutions-adopted-ala-council.

Shannon, Patricia J., Elizabeth Wieling, Jennifer Simmelink-McCleary, and Emily Becher. 2015. "Beyond Stigma: Barriers to Discussing Mental Health in Refugee Populations." *Journal of Loss & Trauma* 20 (3): 281–96. doi:10.1080/15325024.2014.934629.

Shaughnessy, Thomas W. 1972. "The Emerging Environment of the Urban Main Library." *Library Trends* 20 (4): 757–68.

Silva, Elise, and Quinn Galbraith. 2018. "Salary Negotiation Patterns between Women and Men in Academic Libraries." *College and Research Libraries* 79 (3): 324–35. doi:10.5860/crl.79.3.324.

Steiner, Andy. 2018. "New Library Social Worker Will Help Patrons Access Mental Health Supports." *MinnPost.* February 7. https://www.minnpost.com/

mental-health-addiction/2018/02/new-library-social-worker-will-help
-patrons-access-mental-health-sup.

Supiano, Beckie. 2018. "Colleges Teach Students How to Think. Should They
Also Teach Them How to Thrive?" *The Chronicle of Higher Education.*
November 4. https://www.chronicle.com/article/Colleges-Teach-Students
-How-to/244998.

"SWiRSL." 2018. Accessed September 3. https://sites.google.com/nileslibrary
.net/swirsl.

Tervalon, Melanie, and Jann Murray-García. 1998. "Cultural Humility versus
Cultural Competence: A Critical Distinction in Defining Physician Train-
ing Outcomes in Multicultural Education." *Journal of Health Care for the
Poor and Underserved* 9 (2): 117–25.

Trattner, Walter I. 2007. *From Poor Law to Welfare State: A History of Social Welfare
in America.* 6th edition. New York: Simon and Schuster.

Tung, Angela. 2014. "What 21st-Century Libraries Can Learn from This 19th-
Century Institution?" *Quartz.* April 12. https://qz.com/195915/.

U.S. Bureau of Labor Statistics. 2018a. "Librarians: Occupational Outlook Handbook." July 2. https://www.bls.gov/ooh/education-training-and-library/
librarians.htm.

U.S. Bureau of Labor Statistics. 2018b. "Social Workers: Occupational Outlook
Handbook." July 11. https://www.bls.gov/ooh/community-and-social
-service/social-workers.htm.

Useem, Jerry. 2017. "Power Causes Brain Damage." *The Atlantic.* June 18. https://
www.theatlantic.com/magazine/archive/2017/07/power-causes-brain
-damage/528711/.

Index

About the Authors

Sara K. Zettervall, MLIS, MFA, is the founding consultant and trainer at Whole Person Librarianship. She instructs library staff across the nation and the world on applying social work concepts to improve library service, with clients that range from individual libraries to statewide networks. Her experience includes leading community-engaged projects in public, academic, and school libraries and archives. She was the 2017 winner of the Bogle Pratt International Travel Fund in support of presenting with coauthor Mary C. Nienow on library-social work collaboration at the Biennial Symposium of the International Consortium for Social Development in Zagreb, Croatia. Sara has served in the American Library Association for many years, beginning as an LLAMA-sponsored 2014 ALA Emerging Leader and continuing to her current involvement in the Equity, Diversity, and Inclusion Implementation Working Group. She has published on outreach and social justice in *Public Libraries, VOYA, American Libraries, Library Youth Outreach,* and *Progressive Librarian.*

Mary C. Nienow, PhD, is an assistant professor and BSW program director at St. Catherine University (St. Paul, MN). Dr. Nienow has over a decade of experience in research, teaching, advocacy, program coordination, policy development and analysis, and community organizing. She was the cofounder of Grasstops, a nonprofit advocacy organization that assisted nonprofits and small community groups with their policy and advocacy goals. For this work she was awarded the NASW-MN 2006 Early Career Excellence Award. Dr. Nienow's extensive practice experience also includes policy consultant for Hennepin County Medical Center, field director at the University of Wisconsin-Eau Claire, executive director at Child Care WORKS, and lead researcher on Health and Human Services for the Minnesota Senate DFL Caucus. Dr. Nienow's research interests include professional socialization of macro practice social workers, policy and program development, and community-based participatory research.

Discarded